MICROSOFT SWAY

The Complete Tutorial for Beginners

Kiet Huynh

Table of Contents

CHAPTER I
Introduction to Microsoft Sway

1.1 What is Microsoft Sway?

1.1.1 Overview of Sway

Microsoft Sway is a versatile and dynamic presentation tool developed by Microsoft, designed to help users create and share interactive reports, presentations, personal stories, and more. Unlike traditional presentation software like PowerPoint, Sway focuses on simplicity and ease of use while incorporating a range of media and interactive content to enhance the storytelling experience. This overview will cover the essential aspects of Sway, including its purpose, main features, and how it differentiates itself from other presentation tools.

Purpose and Vision

The core purpose of Microsoft Sway is to enable users to create visually appealing, interactive, and easily shareable presentations without needing extensive design skills. Microsoft envisioned Sway as a tool that bridges the gap between professional presentation software and casual storytelling platforms. It caters to a wide audience, including educators, students, business professionals, and personal users, offering a streamlined way to convey information and narratives in a compelling manner.

Key Features of Microsoft Sway

1. Interactive Content Integration:

One of Sway's standout features is its ability to seamlessly integrate various types of interactive content. Users can embed videos, audio clips, images, maps, tweets, and even documents directly into their Sways. This multimedia approach not only enhances the visual appeal but also engages the audience more effectively.

2. Effortless Design and Layout:

Sway simplifies the design process by offering built-in design templates and themes. Users can start with a template and customize it to fit their needs or create a Sway from scratch. The platform automatically adjusts the layout to ensure a cohesive and visually appealing presentation, regardless of the device or screen size.

3. Responsive Design:

Unlike traditional presentation tools that require manual adjustments for different devices, Sway automatically adjusts the layout and design to fit various screen sizes and orientations. This responsive design feature ensures that Sways look great on desktops, tablets, and smartphones without requiring additional effort from the user.

4. Storyline and Design Mode:

Sway provides two main modes for creating and editing content: Storyline and Design. The Storyline mode allows users to focus on the structure and flow of their presentation by arranging cards in a linear sequence. The Design mode offers more advanced customization options, enabling users to tweak the visual aspects of their Sway to achieve the desired look and feel.

5. Collaboration and Sharing:

Collaboration is a key aspect of Sway, allowing multiple users to work on a single Sway simultaneously. This feature is particularly useful for team projects, educational assignments, and business collaborations. Sharing Sways is also straightforward, with options to share via a link, embed on a website, or directly post to social media platforms.

6. Ease of Use:

Microsoft Sway is designed with user-friendliness in mind. Its intuitive interface and drag-and-drop functionality make it accessible to users of all skill levels. Whether you're a seasoned designer or a complete novice, Sway's simplicity ensures that you can create professional-looking presentations without a steep learning curve.

Differentiation from Traditional Presentation Tools

While there are several presentation tools available, Microsoft Sway sets itself apart in various ways. Understanding these differences can help users decide when and why to use Sway over other options.

1. Focus on Content Over Design:

Traditional presentation tools like PowerPoint often require users to spend significant time on design elements, such as aligning text boxes, choosing fonts, and creating animations. Sway, on the other hand, emphasizes content creation and storytelling. The platform's automatic design adjustments allow users to focus on what they want to say, rather than how it looks.

2. Seamless Multimedia Integration:

Sway's ability to embed and integrate a wide range of multimedia content sets it apart from traditional tools. While PowerPoint and similar software can include multimedia, Sway makes the process more seamless and visually integrated, enhancing the overall storytelling experience.

3. Responsive and Adaptive Design:

One of Sway's most significant advantages is its responsive design capability. Traditional tools often require separate adjustments for different devices and screen sizes, whereas Sway automatically adapts to ensure a consistent and visually appealing presentation on any device.

4. Cloud-Based Accessibility:

Sway is entirely cloud-based, meaning users can access and edit their presentations from any device with an internet connection. This feature is particularly beneficial for remote teams, students, and anyone who needs to work on their presentations from multiple locations.

5. Ease of Collaboration:

While traditional tools like PowerPoint have collaboration features, Sway's real-time collaboration capabilities are more seamless and user-friendly. Multiple users can edit a Sway simultaneously, with changes appearing in real-time, making it an excellent choice for collaborative projects.

Use Cases for Microsoft Sway

Microsoft Sway's versatility makes it suitable for a wide range of use cases. Here are some examples of how different users can leverage Sway's features:

1. Education:

- Teachers: Create interactive lessons, educational resources, and classroom presentations that engage students and enhance learning experiences.

- Students: Develop multimedia projects, digital portfolios, and group presentations that showcase their knowledge and creativity.

2. Business:

- Marketing Teams: Design visually compelling marketing materials, product launches, and promotional content that captivate audiences.

- Internal Communications: Share company updates, reports, and training materials in an engaging and easily digestible format.

3. Personal Use:

- Travel Diaries: Document and share travel experiences with friends and family through interactive and visually appealing travel logs.

- Event Planning: Create detailed event plans, invitations, and recaps for personal events like weddings, parties, and reunions.

4. Nonprofits and Community Organizations:

- Awareness Campaigns: Develop interactive and engaging campaigns to raise awareness for causes and encourage community involvement.

- Reports and Updates: Share organizational updates, impact reports, and fundraising results in a compelling format.

Getting Started with Microsoft Sway

To start using Microsoft Sway, you need to have a Microsoft account. Here are the steps to create an account and access Sway:

1. Creating a Microsoft Account:

- Visit the Microsoft account creation page.

- Provide the required information, such as your name, email address, and password.

- Follow the on-screen instructions to verify your email address and complete the account setup.

2. Accessing Sway:

- Once you have a Microsoft account, you can access Sway by visiting the official Sway website (sway.office.com).

- Sign in with your Microsoft account credentials.

- You will be directed to the Sway dashboard, where you can start creating and managing your Sways.

Conclusion

Microsoft Sway is a powerful and user-friendly tool that revolutionizes the way we create and share presentations. Its emphasis on content creation, interactive media integration, and responsive design makes it a valuable asset for educators, business professionals, and personal users alike. By understanding its features and capabilities, you can leverage Sway to craft compelling narratives and presentations that captivate and engage your audience. Whether you're new to presentation tools or looking to enhance your storytelling skills, Microsoft Sway offers the resources and flexibility to bring your ideas to life.

1.1.2 Differences Between Sway and PowerPoint

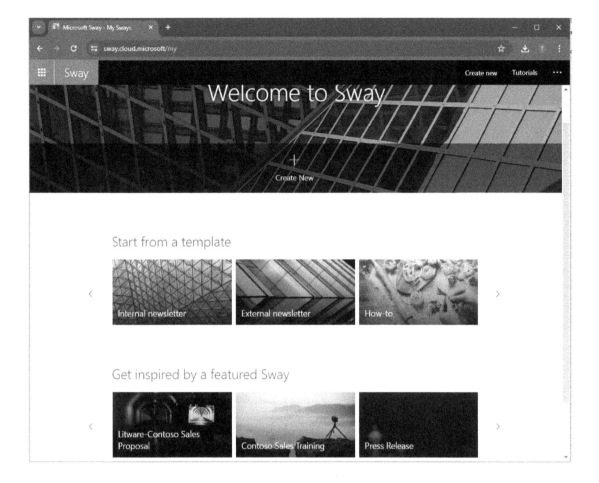

Microsoft Sway and PowerPoint are both powerful tools for creating presentations, but they serve different purposes and excel in various scenarios. Understanding the differences between Sway and PowerPoint can help you decide which tool is best suited for your needs. This section will delve into the fundamental distinctions between these two Microsoft applications, focusing on their unique features, user interfaces, and the types of presentations they are most effective for.

1. User Interface and Design Approach

PowerPoint:

PowerPoint follows a slide-based approach, where each slide can contain various elements such as text, images, charts, and multimedia. The design process in PowerPoint is often manual, requiring users to place and arrange content on individual slides. Users can choose from various templates and themes, but the overall look and feel of the presentation are heavily dependent on the user's design skills. PowerPoint offers extensive formatting options, allowing for detailed customization of every aspect of the slide.

Sway:

Sway, on the other hand, takes a more streamlined approach to design. Instead of slides, Sway uses a storyline composed of different cards. Each card can contain text, images, videos, or other multimedia elements. Sway focuses on the content and allows the design to adapt dynamically. Users add their content, and Sway takes care of the design, ensuring a visually appealing result with minimal effort. Sway's interface is more intuitive for users who are not design experts, making it easy to create professional-looking presentations without in-depth design knowledge.

2. Content Creation and Management

PowerPoint:

In PowerPoint, content creation is more manual and segmented. Users typically add content slide by slide, with each slide acting as a standalone canvas. This approach allows for detailed control over the presentation's flow but can be time-consuming. PowerPoint provides a wide range of tools for creating complex graphics, diagrams, and animations, making it suitable for presentations that require detailed visual content and precise control over every element.

Sway:

Sway simplifies content creation by using cards to build a continuous, flowing narrative. Users add content in a more linear fashion, with each card representing a specific piece of the story. This method is less time-consuming and reduces the need for extensive formatting. Sway's design engine automatically adjusts the layout to ensure consistency and visual appeal. This makes Sway particularly effective for creating content-rich presentations, such as reports, newsletters, and portfolios, where the emphasis is on seamless storytelling.

3. Integration and Collaboration

PowerPoint:

PowerPoint offers robust integration with other Microsoft Office applications and services, such as Excel, Word, and OneDrive. This makes it easy to incorporate data from other sources into your presentations. PowerPoint also supports real-time collaboration, allowing multiple users to work on a presentation simultaneously. This is particularly useful in professional settings where teamwork and iterative feedback are essential.

Sway:

Sway is designed with collaboration and sharing in mind. It integrates seamlessly with cloud services like OneDrive and can pull content from various online sources, including YouTube, Facebook, and Flickr. Sway presentations are stored online by default, making it easy to share them via a link or embed them on websites and social media. Real-time collaboration is also supported, but Sway's cloud-centric nature makes it more accessible for sharing and viewing across different devices.

4. Flexibility and Use Cases

PowerPoint:

PowerPoint is highly versatile and can be used for a wide range of presentation types, from academic lectures and business pitches to detailed training modules and complex project reports. Its extensive customization options make it suitable for any scenario where detailed control over presentation design and content is required.

Sway:

Sway excels in scenarios where the focus is on content over design. It is ideal for creating interactive reports, newsletters, personal stories, portfolios, and lightweight presentations that benefit from a continuous, flowing narrative. Sway's design automation and ease of use make it perfect for users who need to produce polished presentations quickly without spending significant time on formatting.

5. Accessibility and Mobile Experience

PowerPoint:

PowerPoint offers comprehensive accessibility features, including screen reader support, alt text for images, and keyboard shortcuts. PowerPoint presentations can be viewed and edited on various devices, including desktops, tablets, and smartphones, through the PowerPoint app. However, the user experience can vary depending on the device, with more complex editing tasks better suited for desktop use.

Sway:

Sway is designed to be mobile-friendly and responsive. Sway presentations automatically adapt to different screen sizes and orientations, ensuring a consistent viewing experience across desktops, tablets, and smartphones. This makes Sway particularly useful for presentations that will be viewed on mobile devices. Sway also includes accessibility features such as alt text and high contrast modes, ensuring that presentations are accessible to all users.

6. Cost and Availability

PowerPoint:

PowerPoint is available as part of the Microsoft Office suite, which requires a purchase or subscription. While this cost provides access to a wide range of Office applications, it can be a barrier for some users, particularly those who only need presentation software.

Sway:

Sway is available for free with a Microsoft account. There is no standalone cost associated with using Sway, making it an attractive option for users who need a powerful, easy-to-use presentation tool without additional expenses. Sway is included with Office 365 subscriptions, providing additional features and integration options for subscribers.

7. Learning Curve and User Experience

PowerPoint:

PowerPoint has a steeper learning curve due to its extensive features and customization options. Users need to spend time learning how to effectively use the various tools and features to create professional presentations. However, this learning curve is offset by the high degree of control and flexibility that PowerPoint offers.

Sway:

Sway has a much gentler learning curve, with a user-friendly interface that guides users through the content creation process. The focus on simplicity and ease of use makes Sway accessible to beginners and those who need to create presentations quickly without delving into complex design tasks.

Conclusion

In conclusion, while both Microsoft Sway and PowerPoint are powerful tools for creating presentations, they cater to different needs and use cases. PowerPoint is ideal for users who require detailed control over their presentation design and content, making it suitable for complex, highly customized presentations. Sway, on the other hand, offers a streamlined, intuitive approach to content creation, making it perfect for users who need to create visually appealing, content-rich presentations quickly and with minimal effort.

Understanding the key differences between Sway and PowerPoint can help you choose the right tool for your specific needs, ensuring that your presentations are effective, engaging, and well-suited to your audience. Whether you need the detailed customization of PowerPoint or the simplicity and ease of use of Sway, both tools provide valuable capabilities that can enhance your presentations and help you communicate your ideas more effectively.

1.2 Benefits of Using Sway

1.2.1 Interactive Presentations

One of the standout features of Microsoft Sway is its capability to create highly interactive presentations. Unlike traditional slide-based presentation tools, Sway offers a unique approach that enhances user engagement and facilitates a more immersive experience. Interactive presentations are a powerful way to communicate ideas, tell stories, and present information dynamically. In this section, we will explore the various aspects of creating interactive presentations with Sway, highlighting the tools and features that make it possible.

1.2.1.1 Enhancing User Engagement

Interactive presentations are designed to keep the audience engaged. In a traditional presentation, the audience is often passive, simply watching as slides progress. With Sway, the audience becomes an active participant. This engagement is achieved through various interactive elements such as clickable content, embedded media, and interactive navigation.

- Clickable Content: Sway allows you to add clickable elements within your presentation. These can be links to external websites, documents, or other parts of the Sway itself. By enabling the audience to click on elements, you encourage them to explore the content at their own pace and according to their interests.

- Embedded Media: You can embed videos, audio clips, and interactive charts directly into your Sway. This multimedia approach caters to different learning styles and keeps the audience interested. For example, instead of just describing a process, you can include a video demonstration, making the information more accessible and engaging.

- Interactive Navigation: Sway's navigation options are flexible and intuitive. Users can scroll through the content vertically or horizontally, creating a more fluid experience. Additionally, the ability to link to specific sections within the Sway allows for a non-linear presentation format, where users can choose their path through the content.

1.2.1.2 Facilitating Immersive Experiences

Sway's interactive features are not just about keeping the audience engaged but also about creating immersive experiences. This immersive quality is particularly beneficial in educational and training contexts, where deep understanding is crucial.

- Layered Information: With Sway, you can layer information in a way that it unfolds as the user interacts with the presentation. For example, you can present an overview and allow users to click on sections that expand into more detailed explanations. This approach helps in managing information overload and allows users to delve deeper into topics of interest.

- Interactive Maps and Charts: Embedding interactive maps and charts can turn a static presentation into an exploratory experience. For instance, in a geography lesson, you can embed a map where users can click on different regions to learn more about them. Similarly, interactive charts can be used to present data dynamically, where users can interact with the data points to see specific details.

- Quizzes and Polls: Integrating quizzes and polls within your Sway can make the presentation more interactive and educational. These elements can be used to test the audience's knowledge, gather feedback, or stimulate discussion. The immediate feedback from quizzes also helps in reinforcing learning.

1.2.1.3 Customizing the User Experience

One of the strengths of Sway is the ability to customize the user experience to fit the needs of the audience. This customization can be achieved through various design and layout options.

- Responsive Design: Sway presentations are inherently responsive, meaning they adapt to different screen sizes and orientations. This feature ensures that your presentation looks good and functions well on any device, whether it's a desktop, tablet, or smartphone.

- Design Choices: Sway offers a range of design templates and customization options. You can choose from predefined templates or create your own design to match your brand or presentation style. The design elements are intuitive to use, allowing you to focus on the content rather than the formatting.

- Themes and Styles: Sway's themes and styles can be applied to create a consistent look and feel throughout the presentation. You can adjust the color scheme, font styles, and background images to enhance the visual appeal and readability of your content. This level of customization helps in creating a professional and polished presentation.

1.2.1.4 Enhancing Collaboration and Feedback

Interactive presentations with Sway also facilitate collaboration and feedback, which are essential components in both educational and professional settings.

- Collaborative Editing: Sway allows multiple users to collaborate on a presentation in real-time. This feature is particularly useful for group projects or team presentations, where input from various members can be incorporated seamlessly. Collaborative editing ensures that the content is comprehensive and benefits from diverse perspectives.

- Feedback Mechanisms: You can incorporate feedback mechanisms within your Sway presentation. For example, you can add comment sections or feedback forms where users can leave their thoughts and suggestions. This interaction not only enhances the presentation but also provides valuable insights for improvement.

- Live Sharing and Updates: Sway presentations can be shared live with audiences, and any updates made to the presentation are reflected in real-time. This feature is beneficial for ongoing projects or continuous learning modules, where the content evolves over time.

1.2.1.5 Real-World Applications

To understand the practical implications of interactive presentations with Sway, let's explore some real-world applications across different domains.

- Education: In the classroom, teachers can create interactive lessons that keep students engaged. For example, a history teacher can create a Sway presentation on World War II, embedding videos, interactive maps, and quizzes to test students' knowledge. This approach makes learning more dynamic and memorable.

- Business: In the corporate world, interactive presentations can be used for training sessions, marketing pitches, and internal communications. A marketing team can create a Sway presentation to showcase a new product, including interactive elements that allow potential clients to explore features, watch product videos, and fill out interest forms.

- Personal Use: Individuals can use Sway to create personal projects such as travel journals, family newsletters, or event invitations. The interactive elements make these projects more engaging and fun to share with family and friends.

1.2.1.6 Creating Interactive Presentations: Step-by-Step Guide

Let's delve into a step-by-step guide on how to create an interactive presentation with Microsoft Sway.

Step 1: Planning Your Presentation

Before you start creating your Sway, it's essential to plan your presentation. Define the purpose, audience, and key points you want to cover. Consider how you can make the content interactive and engaging.

Step 2: Starting a New Sway

Log in to your Microsoft account and access Sway. Click on "Create New" to start a new Sway. You can choose to start from a template or a blank canvas.

Step 3: Adding Content

Use the "Add Content" button to start building your Sway. Begin with the basics such as text and headings. Gradually add multimedia elements like images, videos, and audio clips. Remember to include interactive elements like links and embedded content.

Step 4: Customizing the Design

Choose a design template that suits your presentation's theme. Customize the design by adjusting colors, fonts, and backgrounds. Use the "Design" and "Styles" tabs to make your Sway visually appealing.

Step 5: Incorporating Interactive Elements

Add interactive elements to your presentation. For instance, you can embed maps, charts, and social media posts. Use the "Embed" option to include external content that users can interact with directly within the Sway.

Step 6: Setting Up Navigation

Configure the navigation to ensure a smooth user experience. Decide whether you want the content to scroll vertically or horizontally. Use the "Navigation" tab to link different sections, creating a non-linear path through your presentation.

Step 7: Sharing and Collaborating

Once your Sway is ready, use the "Share" button to generate a shareable link. Set the permissions to control who can view and edit the presentation. Invite collaborators if you're working on a group project.

Step 8: Gathering Feedback

After sharing your Sway, gather feedback from your audience. Use the built-in feedback forms or encourage comments. Use this feedback to refine and improve your presentation.

Conclusion

Microsoft Sway transforms the way presentations are created and consumed by making them interactive, engaging, and immersive. The interactive elements not only keep the audience engaged but also enhance understanding and retention of the information presented. By leveraging the various tools and features that Sway offers, you can create presentations that are not only informative but also captivating. Whether you are an educator, a business professional, or an individual looking to create compelling presentations, Microsoft Sway provides the perfect platform to bring your ideas to life.

1.2.2 Easy Sharing and Collaboration

The Significance of Easy Sharing in Microsoft Sway

Microsoft Sway is designed to make sharing content as seamless as possible. This ease of sharing is a crucial feature that distinguishes Sway from other presentation tools. In today's interconnected world, the ability to share information effortlessly and collaborate effectively is paramount for productivity and efficiency. Sway's easy sharing capabilities facilitate the distribution of information to a broad audience, whether it's for educational purposes, business presentations, or personal projects.

Sway allows users to share their creations with just a few clicks, without the need for complex processes or additional software. This feature is particularly valuable in environments where quick dissemination of information is necessary, such as in classrooms, business meetings, and remote work scenarios. By simplifying the sharing process, Sway helps users save time and focus on the content rather than the logistics of sharing it.

Sharing Options in Microsoft Sway

Sway offers multiple sharing options to cater to different needs and preferences. Users can share their Sway presentations through direct links, social media platforms, and even embed them into websites. Each of these options provides unique benefits and can be used in various contexts.

Direct Link Sharing

One of the most straightforward ways to share a Sway is by generating a direct link. This method allows users to quickly distribute their presentations to anyone with internet access. The process involves generating a URL that can be copied and pasted into emails, messaging apps, or any other communication platform.

To share a Sway via a direct link, follow these steps:

1. Click on the "Share" button in the upper right corner of the Sway interface.

2. Choose the "Get a link" option.

3. Select the level of access you want to grant (view only, edit, etc.).

4. Click "Create link" and copy the generated URL.

The recipients can then click on the link to view or edit the Sway, depending on the permissions set by the creator. This method is ideal for quick sharing with colleagues, students, or friends without requiring them to log in or create an account.

Social Media Sharing

Sway also integrates with various social media platforms, making it easy to share presentations with a wider audience. Users can post their Sway directly to platforms like Facebook, Twitter, and LinkedIn. This feature is particularly useful for educators who want to share lesson plans with other teachers, businesses that wish to showcase their products or services, and individuals who want to share personal stories or projects with their social media followers.

To share a Sway on social media, follow these steps:

1. Click on the "Share" button in the upper right corner of the Sway interface.

2. Choose the social media platform you want to share your Sway on.

3. Log in to your social media account if prompted.

4. Add a message or description if desired, and then post the Sway.

This method leverages the reach of social media to ensure that the presentation is seen by a broad audience, increasing its visibility and impact.

Embedding Sways

For users who have their own websites or blogs, embedding Sway presentations can be an effective way to enrich their content. Sway provides an embed code that can be inserted into HTML code, allowing the presentation to be viewed directly on a webpage. This feature is particularly useful for content creators, marketers, and educators who want to integrate interactive presentations into their online content.

To embed a Sway, follow these steps:

1. Click on the "Share" button in the upper right corner of the Sway interface.

2. Select the "Embed" option.

3. Customize the size and other settings if necessary.

4. Copy the embed code provided.

5. Paste the embed code into the HTML code of your website or blog.

Embedding Sways ensures that the presentation is easily accessible to website visitors without requiring them to navigate to a separate page. This method enhances user engagement and provides a seamless viewing experience.

Collaborative Features in Microsoft Sway

In addition to easy sharing, Microsoft Sway excels in facilitating collaboration. Collaborative features are essential in today's digital landscape, where teamwork and remote collaboration are increasingly common. Sway's collaborative tools enable multiple users to work on the same presentation simultaneously, streamlining the creation process and fostering a more dynamic and interactive approach to content development.

Inviting Collaborators

One of the core collaborative features of Sway is the ability to invite collaborators to edit a presentation. This feature allows multiple users to contribute to the same Sway, making it ideal for group projects, team presentations, and collaborative content creation. To invite collaborators, follow these steps:

1. Click on the "Share" button in the upper right corner of the Sway interface.

2. Choose the "Invite people to edit" option.

3. Enter the email addresses of the collaborators you want to invite.

4. Customize the invitation message if desired, and then send the invitation.

Collaborators will receive an email invitation with a link to the Sway. They can click on the link to access and edit the presentation, and any changes they make will be automatically saved and visible to all collaborators in real-time. This feature eliminates the need for back-and-forth emails and multiple versions of the same document, making the collaboration process more efficient and organized.

Real-Time Collaboration

Sway supports real-time collaboration, allowing multiple users to edit a presentation simultaneously. This feature is particularly beneficial for teams working on tight deadlines or for projects that require input from various stakeholders. Real-time collaboration ensures that everyone is on the same page and can see the latest updates and changes as they happen.

When collaborating in real-time, users can see who is currently editing the Sway and view their changes in real-time. This transparency fosters a more cohesive and synchronized approach to content creation, reducing the risk of miscommunication and ensuring that the final presentation reflects the collective input and vision of the team.

Comments and Feedback

Another valuable collaborative feature in Sway is the ability to leave comments and feedback. While editing a Sway, collaborators can leave comments on specific sections or elements, providing suggestions, feedback, or additional information. This feature is particularly useful for educators who want to provide feedback on student projects, team members who need to suggest improvements, or clients who need to provide input on a presentation.

To leave a comment, collaborators can highlight the text or element they want to comment on and select the "Comment" option. They can then type their comment and save it. Comments are visible to all collaborators and can be replied to, creating a thread of discussion around specific aspects of the presentation. This feature enhances communication and ensures that all feedback is documented and addressed.

Version History

Sway also includes a version history feature, which allows users to view and revert to previous versions of a presentation. This feature is essential for collaborative projects, as it provides a safety net in case of errors or unintended changes. Users can access the version history to see who made changes and when, and they can restore a previous version if necessary.

To access the version history, follow these steps:

1. Click on the "More options" button (three dots) in the upper right corner of the Sway interface.

2. Select the "Version history" option.

3. Browse through the list of previous versions and select the one you want to restore.

4. Click "Restore" to revert to the selected version.

The version history feature provides peace of mind and ensures that users can easily recover their work if needed. It also promotes accountability by documenting all changes and edits made by collaborators.

Practical Applications of Sway's Sharing and Collaboration Features

The easy sharing and collaboration features of Microsoft Sway have practical applications across various fields and industries. Below are some examples of how these features can be utilized effectively:

Education

In educational settings, Sway's sharing and collaboration features enhance the learning experience for both teachers and students. Teachers can create interactive lesson plans and share them with students via direct links or by embedding them into the class website. Students can collaborate on group projects, with each member contributing their part to a shared Sway. Teachers can leave comments and feedback on student work, providing guidance and suggestions for improvement.

Business

In the business world, Sway's easy sharing and collaboration features streamline the creation and distribution of presentations, reports, and marketing materials. Teams can collaborate on presentations in real-time, ensuring that all members contribute their expertise. Business presentations can be shared with clients and stakeholders via direct links or social media, increasing reach and engagement. The ability to embed Sways into company websites or intranets also enhances internal communication and training.

Personal Use

For personal use, Sway's sharing and collaboration features make it easy to create and share personal projects, such as travel diaries, event invitations, and family newsletters. Users can collaborate with family members or friends to create a shared Sway, with each person adding their photos, stories, and memories. The ability to share Sways via social media or direct links ensures that personal projects can be easily distributed to loved ones.

Conclusion

The easy sharing and collaboration features of Microsoft Sway make it a powerful tool for creating and distributing interactive presentations. By simplifying the sharing process and providing robust collaborative tools, Sway enables users to work together more efficiently and reach a wider audience. Whether used in education, business, or personal projects, Sway's sharing and collaboration features enhance productivity, foster creativity, and streamline communication. As users become more familiar with these features, they can leverage Sway to create impactful and engaging presentations that meet their needs and exceed their expectations.

1.3 Getting Started with Sway

1.3.1 Creating a Microsoft Account

Creating a Microsoft account is the first step in unlocking the full potential of Microsoft Sway. A Microsoft account not only gives you access to Sway but also connects you to a suite of other Microsoft services such as OneDrive, Office Online, and Outlook. This section will guide you through the process of setting up your Microsoft account, ensuring you have the necessary tools to begin creating engaging presentations with Sway.

Why You Need a Microsoft Account

A Microsoft account serves as your gateway to the Microsoft ecosystem. With a single account, you can access various services, including Sway, OneDrive, Office Online, and more. It helps you save and sync your work across multiple devices, ensuring that you can access your presentations anytime, anywhere. Moreover, having a Microsoft account enables you to collaborate with others in real-time, enhancing your productivity and creativity.

Steps to Create a Microsoft Account

Creating a Microsoft account is a straightforward process. Follow these steps to set up your account:

1. Visit the Microsoft Account Creation Page

   - Open your web browser and go to the Microsoft account creation page: https://signup.live.com.

2. Enter Your Information

   - You will be prompted to enter your details, including your first name, last name, and a preferred email address. If you don't have an email address, you can create a new Outlook.com email as part of this process.

- Create a strong password for your account. Make sure it is something you can remember but difficult for others to guess. Microsoft recommends using a mix of uppercase and lowercase letters, numbers, and symbols to enhance security.

3. Verify Your Identity

- Microsoft will ask for additional information to verify your identity. This might include your phone number and an alternate email address. These details are used for account recovery purposes, ensuring you can regain access to your account if you forget your password.

4. Complete the Captcha

- To ensure you are not a robot, you will need to complete a captcha. This step helps Microsoft prevent automated account creation and maintain the security of its services.

5. Agree to the Terms and Conditions

- Review Microsoft's terms and conditions and privacy statement. If you agree, check the box and click the "Next" button to proceed.

6. Verify Your Email Address

- If you used an existing email address, Microsoft will send a verification code to that email. Check your email inbox, retrieve the code, and enter it on the verification page. This step confirms that you have access to the email address you provided.

7. Complete Your Profile

- Once your email address is verified, you will be prompted to complete your profile. This includes adding your birthdate and country/region. Providing accurate information helps Microsoft customize your experience and ensure account security.

8. Final Steps

- After completing your profile, click "Next" to finalize the creation of your Microsoft account. You will be redirected to the Microsoft account dashboard, where you can manage your account settings and access various Microsoft services.

Accessing Your Microsoft Account

Now that you have created your Microsoft account, you can access it anytime by visiting https://account.microsoft.com and signing in with your email address and password. From your account dashboard, you can manage your personal information, security settings, and connected services.

Linking Your Microsoft Account to Sway

With your Microsoft account ready, the next step is to link it to Sway. This is a simple process that ensures you can start creating and managing your presentations seamlessly.

1. Visit the Sway Homepage

  - Open your web browser and go to the Sway homepage: https://sway.office.com.

2. Sign In

  - Click the "Sign in" button located at the top-right corner of the page. Enter the email address and password associated with your Microsoft account.

3. Grant Permissions

  - The first time you sign in to Sway, you may be asked to grant permissions for Sway to access your Microsoft account information. Click "Yes" to allow access. This step is necessary for Sway to save your presentations and sync them with your account.

4. Explore the Sway Dashboard

  - After signing in, you will be taken to the Sway dashboard. Here, you can create new Sways, access your saved presentations, and explore templates and examples.

Setting Up Your Sway Profile

To make the most out of Sway, it's a good idea to set up your Sway profile. This involves personalizing your account and setting preferences that will enhance your user experience.

1. Personal Information

  - Navigate to your profile settings by clicking on your profile picture or initials at the top-right corner of the Sway dashboard and selecting "My Profile." Here, you can update your personal information, such as your name and profile picture.

2. Language and Region Settings

   - Customize your language and region settings to ensure Sway displays information relevant to your location. These settings can be adjusted in the "Settings" section of your Microsoft account dashboard.

3. Notifications

   - Manage your notification preferences to stay informed about updates, collaborations, and other important activities related to your Sways. This can be done through the "Notifications" tab in your profile settings.

Keeping Your Account Secure

Security is paramount when it comes to managing your Microsoft account. Here are some tips to keep your account secure:

1. Enable Two-Factor Authentication

   - Two-factor authentication (2FA) adds an extra layer of security by requiring a second form of verification in addition to your password. Enable 2FA in the "Security" section of your Microsoft account dashboard.

2. Regularly Update Your Password

   - Change your password periodically to reduce the risk of unauthorized access. Use a strong, unique password each time you update it.

3. Monitor Account Activity

   - Keep an eye on your account activity to spot any unusual or unauthorized actions. You can view your recent activity in the "Security" section of your Microsoft account dashboard.

Troubleshooting Account Issues

If you encounter any issues with your Microsoft account, Microsoft provides several resources to help you resolve them:

1. Microsoft Account Help Center

- Visit the Microsoft Account Help Center at https://support.microsoft.com/account for detailed articles and troubleshooting guides on common issues.

2. Contact Support

- If you need personalized assistance, you can contact Microsoft support directly. They offer various support channels, including chat, phone, and email support.

3. Community Forums

- Engage with other users and Microsoft experts in the Microsoft Community Forums. This is a great place to ask questions, share experiences, and find solutions to common problems.

Creating a Microsoft account is a crucial first step in your journey with Microsoft Sway. By following these steps, you ensure that you have access to all the tools and features Sway offers, enabling you to create stunning, interactive presentations with ease. In the next section, we will explore how to access and navigate Sway, setting the stage for your first presentation.

1.3.2 Accessing Sway

Accessing Microsoft Sway is a straightforward process that can be done through various platforms, including web browsers and mobile applications. In this section, we will explore the steps involved in accessing Sway, navigating its interface, and understanding the basic functionalities available to get you started on creating your first Sway.

Accessing Sway via Web Browser

The most common way to access Microsoft Sway is through a web browser. This method is convenient as it does not require any downloads or installations, and you can use Sway from virtually any device with an internet connection. Here's a step-by-step guide to accessing Sway via a web browser:

1. Open Your Web Browser:

   Open your preferred web browser (e.g., Google Chrome, Mozilla Firefox, Microsoft Edge, Safari).

2. Navigate to the Sway Website:

   Type the following URL into your browser's address bar: sway.office.com. Press Enter to navigate to the Sway homepage.

3. Sign In to Your Microsoft Account:

   - If you already have a Microsoft account, click on the "Sign in" button located at the top right corner of the page.

   - Enter your Microsoft account email address and password.

   - If you do not have a Microsoft account, click on "Create one" and follow the prompts to set up a new account.

4. Access the Sway Dashboard:

   After signing in, you will be directed to the Sway dashboard. Here, you can see all your existing Sways and options to create new ones.

Accessing Sway via Mobile Applications

Microsoft Sway also offers mobile applications for both iOS and Android devices, allowing you to create and edit Sways on the go. To access Sway via a mobile app, follow these steps:

1. Download the Sway App:

   - For iOS devices, open the App Store and search for "Microsoft Sway."

   - For Android devices, open the Google Play Store and search for "Microsoft Sway."

   - Download and install the app on your device.

2. Open the Sway App:

   Once the app is installed, tap on the Sway icon to open it.

3. Sign In to Your Microsoft Account:

   - If you already have a Microsoft account, enter your email address and password to sign in.

   - If you do not have a Microsoft account, follow the prompts to create one.

4. Explore the Mobile Interface:

   The mobile app interface is designed to be user-friendly, with similar functionalities to the web version. You can create, edit, and view Sways directly from your mobile device.

Navigating the Sway Interface

Once you have accessed Sway, understanding the interface is crucial for efficiently creating and managing your presentations. The Sway interface is divided into several key areas:

1. The Dashboard:

   The dashboard is your main hub in Sway. Here, you can:

   - View your existing Sways.

   - Create new Sways.

   - Access templates for different types of presentations.

   - Open shared Sways.

   - Manage your account settings.

2. The Storyline:

The Storyline is where you build the content of your Sway. It is a linear sequence of cards, each representing a piece of content such as text, images, videos, or embedded media. The Storyline area allows you to:

- Add new cards by clicking on the "+" button.

- Rearrange cards by dragging and dropping them.

- Edit the content of each card directly.

3. The Design Tab:

The Design tab is where you customize the appearance of your Sway. You can:

- Choose a design style from the available themes.

- Customize the color scheme and fonts.

- Preview how your Sway will look to viewers.

4. The Navigation Pane:

The navigation pane helps you move through your Sway efficiently. It shows a thumbnail view of all your cards, allowing you to quickly jump to specific sections.

Creating Your First Sway

Now that you know how to access and navigate the Sway interface, let's create your first Sway. Follow these steps to get started:

1. Start a New Sway:

- From the dashboard, click on "Create New" to start a blank Sway, or choose a template to start with a pre-designed layout.

2. Add Content to the Storyline:

- Click on the "+" button to add a new card.

- Select the type of content you want to add, such as text, image, video, or embedded content.

- Fill in the content for each card. For example, if you are adding a text card, type your text into the provided field.

3. Customize the Design:

   - Switch to the Design tab.

   - Choose a design style that matches the theme of your presentation.

   - Customize the color scheme and fonts to match your preferences.

4. Preview Your Sway:

   - Click on the "Play" button to preview your Sway.

   - Review each section to ensure everything looks as expected.

5. Save and Share Your Sway:

   - Click on "Save" to ensure your changes are preserved.

   - To share your Sway, click on the "Share" button and choose the sharing settings that suit your needs. You can generate a shareable link, invite specific people, or embed your Sway in a website.

Tips for Effective Sway Presentations

To make the most out of Microsoft Sway, consider the following tips for creating effective and engaging presentations:

1. Plan Your Content:

   Before you start building your Sway, outline the key points you want to cover. This will help you organize your content logically and ensure that you include all necessary information.

2. Use High-Quality Media:

   Incorporate high-quality images and videos to make your Sway visually appealing. Avoid using low-resolution media that can detract from the overall presentation.

3. Keep It Simple:

While it's tempting to add a lot of content, keeping your Sway concise and focused will make it more impactful. Use clear headings and bullet points to break up text and highlight key points.

4. Leverage Interactive Elements:

Sway allows you to embed interactive elements such as maps, social media posts, and forms. Use these features to make your presentation more engaging and interactive for your audience.

5. Test on Different Devices:

Preview your Sway on different devices (desktop, tablet, mobile) to ensure it looks good and functions properly across various platforms.

Troubleshooting Common Issues

While Microsoft Sway is designed to be user-friendly, you may encounter some common issues. Here are solutions to a few common problems:

1. Issue: Difficulty Signing In

  - Ensure you are using the correct Microsoft account credentials.

  - If you've forgotten your password, use the "Forgot password" link to reset it.

2. Issue: Media Not Uploading

  - Check your internet connection to ensure it's stable.

  - Ensure the file size and format are supported by Sway.

  - Try uploading the media again after refreshing your browser or restarting the app.

3. Issue: Sway Not Displaying Correctly on Mobile Devices

  - Make sure your mobile app is up to date.

  - Check the design settings to ensure your Sway is optimized for mobile viewing.

  - Adjust the layout if necessary to improve the mobile viewing experience.

4. Issue: Sharing Settings Not Working

  - Verify that you have set the correct sharing permissions.

- Ensure the recipients have access to view the shared link.

- If embedding, check that the embed code is correctly inserted on your website or platform.

Conclusion

Accessing and using Microsoft Sway is a seamless process that empowers you to create dynamic and interactive presentations. Whether you are using it through a web browser or a mobile app, the intuitive interface and powerful features of Sway make it an excellent tool for a variety of presentation needs. By following the steps and tips outlined in this section, you can confidently start creating your own engaging Sways and leverage the full potential of this innovative platform.

In the next chapters, we will delve deeper into advanced features, design customization, and specific use cases to help you master Microsoft Sway and take your presentations to the next level. Stay tuned as we continue to explore the many capabilities of this versatile tool.

CHAPTER II
Navigating the Sway Interface

2.1 Overview of the Sway Dashboard

The Sway Dashboard is your central hub for creating, managing, and accessing all of your Sway projects. It offers a clean, user-friendly interface designed to make the process of digital storytelling as seamless as possible. The Dashboard is divided into several key areas, each with specific functions and features that help you navigate through your Sways efficiently.

When you first log into Microsoft Sway, you are greeted by the Dashboard. This is the place where you can see all of your existing Sways, start a new project, or explore various templates and examples. Understanding the layout and features of the Dashboard is crucial for getting the most out of Sway.

2.1.1 Home Screen

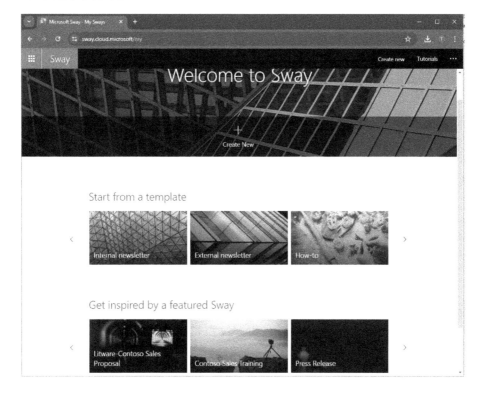

The Home Screen of the Sway Dashboard is the first thing you see upon logging in. It serves as the starting point for all your Sway activities. Let's delve into the components and functionalities of the Home Screen in detail:

1. Navigation Bar:

At the top of the Home Screen, you will find the Navigation Bar. This bar includes links to other Microsoft Office apps, notifications, your profile settings, and the main menu for Sway. The Navigation Bar is always accessible, no matter where you are within Sway, providing quick access to essential features and settings.

2. Create New Sway:

Prominently displayed on the Home Screen is the "Create New" button. This is your gateway to starting a new Sway project. Clicking this button gives you the option to start from a blank canvas, use a template, or import content from an existing document such as a Word file or a PDF. This flexibility allows users of all skill levels to begin their projects easily.

3. Featured Sways:

Just below the "Create New" button, you will often see a selection of Featured Sways. These are examples of what you can achieve with Sway and are curated by Microsoft to inspire users. Browsing through these featured projects can provide ideas and best practices for your own Sway creations.

4. My Sways:

This section displays all the Sways you have created or are currently working on. The Sways are usually presented in a grid or list format, showing thumbnails for easy identification. Each Sway in this section provides quick actions such as editing, sharing, or deleting. The "My Sways" section is an efficient way to manage your projects, allowing you to quickly locate and access your work.

5. Templates:

To the right of the "Create New" button, you will find the Templates section. Templates in Sway are pre-designed layouts that you can use as a starting point for your projects. They are categorized based on use cases such as business presentations, educational reports, personal stories, and more. Templates can save you time and effort, especially if you are new to Sway or need inspiration.

6. Recent Documents:

If you have recently worked on Sway projects, they will appear in the Recent Documents section. This provides a quick way to jump back into your recent work without having to search through the "My Sways" section. It is particularly useful for ongoing projects that require frequent updates.

7. Search Bar:

At the top of the "My Sways" section, there is a search bar that allows you to search for specific Sways by title or keywords. This feature is especially useful if you have a large number of Sways and need to find a particular project quickly.

8. Help and Support:

Located at the bottom of the Home Screen, you will find links to Help and Support resources. These include tutorials, FAQs, and contact information for Microsoft Support.

This section is invaluable for new users who need guidance or encounter issues while using Sway.

9. Profile and Settings:

In the upper right corner of the Home Screen, you will find your profile icon. Clicking on this icon reveals options for accessing your Microsoft account settings, updating your profile, and signing out of Sway. Managing your profile settings is important for ensuring that your Sway experience is personalized and secure.

Understanding the Navigation Bar

The Navigation Bar is a persistent feature at the top of the Sway Dashboard. It ensures that you can access important functions regardless of where you are within the application. Here's a closer look at its components:

- Microsoft Office Apps: On the left side of the Navigation Bar, you'll find icons for other Microsoft Office apps such as Word, Excel, PowerPoint, and OneDrive. Clicking these icons allows you to switch between different Office applications seamlessly, making it easy to integrate Sway with your other Office tools.

- Notifications: The bell icon represents your notifications. Any updates, alerts, or messages related to your Sway account or projects will appear here. Keeping an eye on notifications helps you stay informed about collaboration requests, updates to shared Sways, and other important events.

- Main Menu: The hamburger menu (three horizontal lines) on the left side opens the main menu for Sway. This menu includes options like creating a new Sway, accessing templates, viewing your Sways, and exploring featured content. It provides an alternative navigation method to the main sections of the Dashboard.

Creating a New Sway

When you click on the "Create New" button, you are presented with several options for starting your project:

- Blank Sway: Start from scratch with a blank canvas. This option gives you full creative freedom to build your Sway from the ground up.

- Template: Choose from a variety of pre-designed templates. Templates are categorized based on their intended use, such as business reports, portfolios, newsletters, and educational materials.

- Import: You can import content from existing documents, such as Word files, PDFs, or even other Sways. This feature is particularly useful if you have pre-written content or if you want to convert an existing document into a more dynamic Sway presentation.

Featured Sways

Featured Sways are curated examples provided by Microsoft to showcase the capabilities of the platform. Browsing through these examples can give you a sense of what's possible with Sway. Each featured Sway includes a preview that you can click on to explore the full content. These examples cover a wide range of topics and styles, demonstrating the versatility of Sway in creating engaging, interactive content.

Managing Your Sways

The "My Sways" section is your personal library of all the Sway projects you have created or collaborated on. Each Sway is represented by a thumbnail that provides a visual cue about the content. The thumbnails make it easy to identify your projects at a glance. Next to each Sway, you'll find options to:

- Edit: Opens the Sway in edit mode, allowing you to make changes to the content and design.

- Share: Provides sharing options, including generating a shareable link or inviting collaborators.

- Delete: Removes the Sway from your library. Deleted Sways may be moved to a recycle bin where they can be restored if needed.

Using Templates

Templates are a great way to jumpstart your Sway projects. Each template is designed with a specific purpose in mind, and includes pre-formatted content blocks that you can customize. This saves you time and ensures that your Sway has a professional look and feel from the start. Templates are organized into categories such as:

- Business: Professional presentations, reports, and newsletters.

- Education: Lesson plans, student projects, and educational reports.

- Personal: Stories, event invitations, and photo albums.

Recent Documents

The Recent Documents section displays your most recently accessed Sways. This makes it easy to continue working on ongoing projects without having to search for them. Each entry includes a thumbnail and the last modified date, giving you quick access to your most current work.

Search Functionality

The search bar is a powerful tool for finding specific Sways. By entering keywords or titles, you can quickly locate the Sway you need. This is especially useful if you have a large collection of Sways and need to find a particular project quickly.

Help and Support

The Help and Support section is your go-to resource for assistance with Sway. It includes links to:

- Tutorials: Step-by-step guides and videos to help you learn how to use Sway effectively.

- FAQs: Answers to common questions about Sway's features and functionality.

- Contact Support: Information on how to contact Microsoft Support for personalized assistance.

Profile and Settings

Your profile icon in the upper right corner of the Home Screen provides access to your account settings. Here, you can update your profile information, change your password, and manage your subscription settings. Ensuring your profile is up-to-date helps personalize your Sway experience and keeps your account secure.

2.1.2 My Sways

The "My Sways" section is an essential part of the Sway dashboard, providing users with a centralized location to manage all their Sway presentations. This section ensures that users can efficiently organize, access, and track their Sway projects, making it an indispensable tool for both beginners and seasoned users. In this section, we'll delve into the various features and functionalities of the "My Sways" section to help you leverage its full potential.

Accessing "My Sways"

To access the "My Sways" section, you need to log in to your Microsoft Sway account. Once logged in, you'll be directed to the main dashboard, where you'll find the "My Sways" tab prominently displayed. Clicking on this tab will take you to a page that showcases all your Sway projects in a neatly organized manner.

Understanding the Layout

The "My Sways" page is designed for ease of use, with a clean and intuitive layout. At the top, you'll find a search bar, which allows you to quickly find specific Sways by typing in keywords or titles. Below the search bar, you'll see a series of options to filter and sort your Sways, including sorting by date created, date modified, and alphabetical order.

Sway Thumbnails

Each Sway project is represented by a thumbnail image, which provides a visual cue of the content within. These thumbnails are automatically generated based on the design and content of each Sway, giving you an immediate sense of what each presentation entails. Hovering over a thumbnail reveals additional options, such as previewing the Sway, editing it, sharing it, or deleting it.

Organizing Your Sways

As your collection of Sway presentations grows, organization becomes crucial. The "My Sways" section offers several tools to help you keep your projects orderly:

- Folders: You can create folders to group related Sways together. For instance, you might have folders for work presentations, school projects, personal stories, etc. To create a folder, click on the "New Folder" button, name your folder, and then drag and drop your Sways into the appropriate folders.

- Tags: Another way to organize your Sways is by using tags. Tags are keywords or phrases that you can assign to each Sway to help categorize them. For example, you might tag Sways with terms like "Marketing," "Education," or "Travel." You can then use the search bar to filter Sways by these tags, making it easier to find related presentations.

- Favorites: If you have certain Sways that you frequently access, you can mark them as favorites. This will pin them to the top of the "My Sways" page, ensuring quick and easy access.

Managing Sway Details

Each Sway in the "My Sways" section comes with a set of management options that allow you to handle various aspects of your presentations:

- Edit: Clicking the edit option takes you directly into the Sway editor, where you can make changes to the content, design, and layout of your presentation.

- Share: The share option provides several ways to distribute your Sway. You can generate a shareable link, invite collaborators by email, or share directly to social media platforms.

- Duplicate: If you need to create a new Sway based on an existing one, you can use the duplicate option. This creates a copy of the selected Sway, allowing you to make modifications without altering the original.

- Delete: If you no longer need a particular Sway, you can delete it from your collection. It's important to note that deleted Sways are moved to the "Deleted Sways" section, where they can be restored if needed.

Collaborating on Sways

One of the powerful features of Microsoft Sway is the ability to collaborate with others. The "My Sways" section makes it easy to manage collaboration on your presentations.

- Inviting Collaborators: To invite collaborators, select the Sway you want to share, click on the share option, and choose "Invite people to edit." You can then enter the email addresses of the collaborators, who will receive an invitation to join and edit the Sway.

- Managing Permissions: You can control the level of access each collaborator has. Options include allowing them to view, edit, or have full control over the Sway, including the ability to invite additional collaborators.

- Tracking Changes: As collaborators make changes to the Sway, you can track these changes in real-time. The "My Sways" section will display updates and modifications, ensuring that everyone stays on the same page.

Searching and Filtering Sways

The "My Sways" section includes robust search and filtering capabilities to help you quickly locate specific presentations:

- Search Bar: Enter keywords, phrases, or titles into the search bar to find matching Sways. The search functionality is smart and can return results based on content within the Sway, not just the title.

- Filters: Use filters to narrow down your Sways based on criteria like date created, date modified, and tags. This is particularly useful when you have a large number of Sways and need to find something specific quickly.

Advanced Features

For users who want to take full advantage of the "My Sways" section, there are several advanced features worth exploring:

- Version History: If you're working on a Sway with multiple collaborators, keeping track of changes can be challenging. Sway offers version history, allowing you to see previous versions of your Sway and revert to an earlier version if needed.

- Analytics: Understanding how your Sway is being received by viewers can provide valuable insights. Sway provides basic analytics, such as the number of views, average viewing time, and more. These metrics can help you gauge the effectiveness of your presentations and identify areas for improvement.

- Accessibility: Ensuring your Sways are accessible to all viewers is crucial. The "My Sways" section includes tools for checking and improving accessibility, such as adding alt text to images, ensuring proper heading structures, and more.

Best Practices for Managing Sways

To make the most out of the "My Sways" section, consider the following best practices:

- Regularly Review and Update: Periodically review your Sways to ensure they are up to date. Remove outdated or unnecessary Sways to keep your collection manageable.

- Consistent Naming Conventions: Use consistent naming conventions for your Sways to make them easier to find. For example, you might start each Sway title with a project name or date.

- Backup Important Sways: While Sway offers cloud storage, it's a good idea to backup important Sways by exporting them to PDF or saving them in another format.

Troubleshooting Common Issues

Even with a user-friendly interface, you might encounter some issues while managing your Sways:

- Missing Sways: If a Sway appears to be missing, check the "Deleted Sways" section. If it was accidentally deleted, you can restore it from there.

- Slow Performance: If the "My Sways" section is slow to load, try clearing your browser cache or using a different browser. Performance issues can sometimes be related to browser settings or extensions.

- Collaborator Access Problems: If a collaborator is having trouble accessing a Sway, ensure they have the correct permissions. Resending the invitation can also resolve access issues.

Conclusion

The "My Sways" section is a powerful tool for managing your Sway presentations. By understanding its features and functionalities, you can keep your Sways organized, collaborate effectively, and ensure your presentations are always accessible and up to date. Whether you're creating Sways for work, school, or personal projects, mastering the "My Sways" section will enhance your overall Sway experience.

By following the tips and best practices outlined in this section, you'll be well-equipped to manage your Sway presentations efficiently and effectively, making the most of all the tools and features that Microsoft Sway has to offer.

2.2 The Storyline and Design Tabs

The Storyline is one of the most critical components of Microsoft Sway, serving as the backbone of your presentation or document. It is the area where you build, organize, and structure your content. Unlike traditional presentation tools that rely heavily on slide decks, Sway uses the Storyline to offer a more fluid, dynamic, and interactive approach to content creation. This section will guide you through understanding the Storyline, how to effectively use it, and the benefits it offers.

2.2.1 Understanding the Storyline

Introduction to the Storyline

The Storyline in Microsoft Sway can be thought of as a linear storyboard where you piece together different content blocks called "cards." These cards can contain various types of media and information, such as text, images, videos, and embedded content. Each card represents a distinct element of your presentation, and together they form a coherent and engaging narrative.

The Concept of Cards

In the Storyline, everything revolves around cards. These are the building blocks of your Sway. Cards can be of several types, each designed to accommodate different kinds of content:

1. Text Cards: These are used for adding text content. You can format the text, create headings, and add emphasis through bold or italic styles.

2. Media Cards: These include image, video, and audio cards. Media cards allow you to insert multimedia content to make your Sway more engaging.

3. Group Cards: These are used to organize multiple cards together. Group cards can be formatted in various styles, such as grids or stacks, to present related content cohesively.

4. Embed Cards: These allow you to embed interactive content from other web services, such as maps, charts, social media posts, and more.

Adding and Managing Cards

To add a card to your Storyline, simply click the plus (+) icon located at the bottom of any existing card. This action will open a menu where you can select the type of card you wish to add. Here's how you can manage the different aspects of cards:

- Adding Text Cards: Click on the text option in the menu, and a new text card will appear in the Storyline. You can then type your content directly into the card and use the formatting toolbar to adjust the appearance.

- Adding Media Cards: Select the media type (image, video, or audio) from the menu. You can then upload your own media or search for it online using the built-in search functionality.

- Organizing Cards: Drag and drop cards within the Storyline to rearrange their order. This flexibility allows you to structure your narrative in the most logical and impactful way.

Customizing the Storyline

Customization is a significant aspect of using the Storyline effectively. Here are some tips to help you get the most out of your Storyline:

1. Using Headers: Headers help break down the content into sections, making it easier for your audience to follow. You can add headers by selecting the "Header" option from the card menu.

2. Grouping Cards: Use group cards to combine related content. For instance, you can create a group card to showcase a gallery of images or a collection of related text cards.

3. Backgrounds and Emphasis: Customize the appearance of individual cards by changing their background or emphasizing key points. This can be done through the card's formatting options.

Storyline Versus Traditional Slide Decks

One of the significant advantages of Sway's Storyline over traditional slide decks is the fluidity and interactivity it offers. Traditional slides are static and often linear, whereas Sway's Storyline allows for a more engaging experience. Here are some key differences:

1. Fluid Navigation: The Storyline enables users to navigate through content in a non-linear fashion. This fluidity is particularly useful for interactive presentations where the audience can explore different sections at their own pace.

2. Dynamic Content: Unlike static slides, the Storyline supports dynamic content such as live feeds and embedded interactive elements. This makes your presentation more engaging and up-to-date.

3. Ease of Use: Sway's intuitive interface makes it easy to add and organize content. The drag-and-drop functionality and card-based system simplify the content creation process compared to traditional slide software.

Best Practices for Using the Storyline

To make the most out of the Storyline, consider the following best practices:

1. Plan Your Content: Before adding cards, plan the structure of your presentation. Decide on the main sections and the type of content you will include.

2. Maintain a Logical Flow: Ensure that the sequence of cards follows a logical flow. This helps your audience understand and engage with the content more effectively.

3. Use Multimedia Wisely: While multimedia can enhance your presentation, avoid overloading your Sway with too many images or videos. Strike a balance to maintain the audience's attention.

4. Engage with Interactive Elements: Incorporate interactive elements such as embedded maps, social media posts, or quizzes to make your Sway more engaging.

Conclusion

Understanding the Storyline is crucial for creating effective and engaging content in Microsoft Sway. By leveraging the flexibility and dynamic nature of cards, you can build presentations that are not only informative but also visually appealing and interactive. The key to mastering the Storyline lies in experimenting with different card types, customizing your content, and maintaining a logical flow throughout your presentation. As you become more familiar with these features, you will find that Microsoft Sway offers a powerful and versatile platform for all your content creation needs.

2.2.2 Exploring the Design Tab

The Design tab in Microsoft Sway is where you can bring your creative vision to life. This tab allows you to customize the look and feel of your Sway, making it visually appealing and engaging for your audience. Understanding and effectively using the Design tab is crucial for creating professional and attractive presentations. This section will guide you through the various features and options available in the Design tab, helping you to explore its full potential.

Introduction to the Design Tab

When you switch to the Design tab in Microsoft Sway, you are presented with a variety of customization options that enable you to enhance the visual appeal of your presentation. The Design tab is divided into several sections, each offering different tools and settings to tweak the appearance of your Sway. These sections include Styles, Customize, Navigation, and Accessibility.

Styles

The Styles section in the Design tab allows you to choose from a range of predefined themes that set the overall look of your Sway. These themes include different color schemes, fonts, and layout styles. Selecting a theme is the first step in designing your Sway, as it provides a cohesive visual structure that you can build upon.

Choosing a Theme

1. Predefined Themes: Microsoft Sway offers a variety of predefined themes that are designed to suit different types of content. These themes automatically apply a combination of colors, fonts, and layout settings to your Sway. To choose a theme, simply click on one of the options displayed in the Styles section. You can preview how each theme will look on your Sway before making a final decision.

2. Custom Themes: If the predefined themes do not meet your requirements, you can create a custom theme. Custom themes allow you to select specific colors, fonts, and layouts that align with your branding or personal preferences. To create a custom theme, click on the "Customize" option in the Styles section, and follow the prompts to select your desired settings.

Color Schemes

1. Default Colors: Each predefined theme comes with a default color scheme that is carefully chosen to complement the overall design. These default colors ensure that your Sway looks professional and visually appealing.

2. Custom Colors: If you want to use specific colors that are not included in the default schemes, you can customize the color palette. Click on the "Colors" option in the Customize section and choose from a range of colors or input specific color codes to match your branding or personal preferences.

Fonts

1. Default Fonts: Similar to color schemes, each predefined theme includes a set of default fonts. These fonts are selected to ensure readability and consistency across your Sway.

2. Custom Fonts: If you prefer to use different fonts, you can customize the typography of your Sway. Click on the "Fonts" option in the Customize section and choose from a variety of fonts available in the Sway library.

Customize

The Customize section in the Design tab allows you to fine-tune the visual elements of your Sway. This section provides options to adjust the layout, animation, and other design elements to create a unique and engaging presentation.

Layout Options

1. Vertical Layout: The vertical layout arranges your content in a continuous, scrolling format. This layout is ideal for presentations that are meant to be viewed on mobile devices or for creating long-form content.

2. Horizontal Layout: The horizontal layout arranges your content in a series of horizontal slides. This layout is similar to traditional slide-based presentations and is suitable for content that is meant to be viewed on larger screens.

3. Grid Layout: The grid layout arranges your content in a grid format, allowing you to display multiple pieces of content side by side. This layout is useful for creating visually rich presentations with multiple media elements.

Animation and Transitions

1. Animation Styles: Sway offers several animation styles that add movement and interactivity to your presentation. These animations can be applied to individual cards or to the entire Sway. To choose an animation style, click on the "Animations" option in the Customize section and select from the available options.

2. Transition Effects: Transition effects control how your Sway moves from one section to another. These effects can enhance the flow of your presentation and make it more engaging. To choose a transition effect, click on the "Transitions" option in the Customize section and select from the available options.

Background Images

1. Default Backgrounds: Each predefined theme comes with a default background image or color. These backgrounds are selected to complement the overall design of the theme.

2. Custom Backgrounds: If you want to use a specific background image or color, you can customize the background of your Sway. Click on the "Background" option in the Customize section and choose from the available images or upload your own.

Navigation

The Navigation section in the Design tab allows you to customize how users navigate through your Sway. This section provides options to adjust the navigation style, add navigation aids, and customize the navigation bar.

Navigation Style

1. Default Navigation: The default navigation style is determined by the layout you choose. For example, the vertical layout uses a scrolling navigation style, while the horizontal layout uses a slide-based navigation style.

2. Custom Navigation: If you want to customize the navigation style, click on the "Navigation" option in the Navigation section and choose from the available options. You can select from different navigation styles, such as continuous scrolling, slide-based navigation, or grid-based navigation.

Navigation Aids

1. Table of Contents: The table of contents provides a quick overview of the sections in your Sway and allows users to jump to specific sections. To add a table of contents, click on the

"Table of Contents" option in the Navigation section and follow the prompts to customize its appearance.

2. Section Markers: Section markers divide your Sway into distinct sections and help users navigate through your presentation. To add section markers, click on the "Section Markers" option in the Navigation section and follow the prompts to customize their appearance.

Navigation Bar

1. Default Navigation Bar: The default navigation bar is determined by the layout and theme you choose. It provides basic navigation controls, such as next and previous buttons.

2. Custom Navigation Bar: If you want to customize the navigation bar, click on the "Navigation Bar" option in the Navigation section and choose from the available options. You can add custom navigation controls, such as a progress indicator or a custom menu.

Accessibility

The Accessibility section in the Design tab allows you to ensure that your Sway is accessible to all users, including those with disabilities. This section provides options to add alt text, use high contrast mode, and customize the accessibility settings of your Sway.

Adding Alt Text

1. Alt Text for Images: Alt text provides a text description of images, which is read aloud by screen readers for users with visual impairments. To add alt text to an image, click on the image and select the "Alt Text" option. Enter a brief description of the image in the text box provided.

2. Alt Text for Videos: Similar to images, alt text can also be added to videos. To add alt text to a video, click on the video and select the "Alt Text" option. Enter a brief description of the video in the text box provided.

High Contrast Mode

1. Enabling High Contrast Mode: High contrast mode increases the contrast between text and background, making it easier for users with visual impairments to read the content. To enable high contrast mode, click on the "High Contrast Mode" option in the Accessibility section and follow the prompts to customize its appearance.

2. Customizing High Contrast Mode: You can customize the appearance of high contrast mode by selecting different color schemes and text styles. To customize high contrast

mode, click on the "Customize" option in the High Contrast Mode section and choose from the available options.

Customizing Accessibility Settings

1. Accessibility Checker: The accessibility checker scans your Sway for potential accessibility issues and provides suggestions for improvement. To use the accessibility checker, click on the "Accessibility Checker" option in the Accessibility section and follow the prompts to review and address any issues.

2. Custom Accessibility Settings: You can customize the accessibility settings of your Sway to meet specific needs. To customize the accessibility settings, click on the "Accessibility Settings" option in the Accessibility section and choose from the available options.

Conclusion

Exploring the Design tab in Microsoft Sway allows you to create visually appealing and engaging presentations that captivate your audience. By understanding and effectively using the various customization options available in the Design tab, you can enhance the look and feel of your Sway, ensuring that it meets your specific needs and preferences. Whether you are creating a presentation for educational purposes, business use, or personal projects, the Design tab provides the tools and settings to bring your creative vision to life.

2.3 Using the Navigation Pane

Navigating through the Sway interface efficiently is crucial for creating dynamic and engaging presentations. The navigation pane in Sway is a powerful tool that allows you to manage and structure your content seamlessly. In this section, we'll delve into the details of navigating through Sway cards, which are the building blocks of your presentation.

2.3.1 Navigating Through Sway Cards

Sway cards are the fundamental elements that make up your Sway presentation. Each card can contain different types of content such as text, images, videos, and more. Navigating through these cards effectively is essential for ensuring that your presentation flows logically and engages your audience. Let's explore the various aspects of navigating through Sway cards.

Understanding Sway Cards

Before diving into the navigation, it's important to understand the different types of Sway cards and their purposes. Sway offers a variety of cards to cater to different content needs:

1. Text Cards: These are used for adding text content. You can format the text using various styles, such as headings, subheadings, and paragraphs.

2. Media Cards: These include image cards, video cards, and audio cards. They allow you to incorporate multimedia elements into your presentation.

3. Group Cards: These are used to group multiple cards together, such as stack cards, grid cards, and slideshow cards. Group cards help in organizing related content efficiently.

4. Embed Cards: These cards allow you to embed external content like maps, social media posts, and websites directly into your Sway.

Accessing and Navigating Cards

To begin navigating through Sway cards, follow these steps:

1. Opening the Navigation Pane: The navigation pane can be accessed by clicking on the icon located on the left side of the Sway interface. This pane provides an overview of all the cards in your Sway, organized in a sequential order.

2. Viewing Card Thumbnails: Once the navigation pane is open, you'll see thumbnails of all your Sway cards. This visual representation helps you quickly identify and locate specific cards within your presentation.

3. Scrolling Through Cards: Use the scroll bar or your mouse wheel to scroll through the list of cards. This is particularly useful when your Sway contains a large number of cards.

4. Selecting a Card: Click on any card thumbnail to navigate directly to that card. This will bring the selected card into the main editing area, where you can make changes or view its content in detail.

5. Expanding and Collapsing Groups: If you're using group cards, you can expand or collapse these groups to manage your content more efficiently. Click on the arrow next to the group card thumbnail to expand or collapse the group.

Reordering Cards

Reordering cards is a key aspect of navigation that allows you to control the flow of your presentation. Here's how you can reorder cards in Sway:

1. Drag and Drop: To move a card, click and hold the card thumbnail in the navigation pane, then drag it to the desired position. Release the mouse button to drop the card into place. This simple drag-and-drop functionality makes it easy to rearrange your content.

2. Keyboard Shortcuts: For users who prefer keyboard shortcuts, Sway offers options to move cards up or down in the order. Select the card you want to move and use the keyboard shortcuts to reposition it.

3. Reordering Groups: When dealing with group cards, you can reorder the entire group or individual cards within the group. Drag and drop the group card to move the entire group, or expand the group and drag individual cards to reorder them within the group.

Duplicating and Deleting Cards

Managing your content also involves duplicating and deleting cards. These actions are part of efficient navigation and content management:

1. Duplicating Cards: To duplicate a card, right-click on the card thumbnail in the navigation pane and select "Duplicate." This creates a copy of the selected card, which can be edited independently of the original.

2. Deleting Cards: To delete a card, right-click on the card thumbnail and select "Delete." Confirm the deletion if prompted. Deleting unnecessary cards helps in keeping your Sway clean and focused.

Navigating Between Sections

In addition to individual cards, Sway presentations often include sections that group related cards together. Navigating between these sections is another crucial aspect of managing your Sway:

1. Section Headers: Sections are marked by headers in the navigation pane. These headers help in identifying the beginning of each section.

2. Expanding and Collapsing Sections: Similar to group cards, sections can be expanded or collapsed. Click on the arrow next to the section header to expand or collapse the section, making it easier to navigate large presentations.

3. Jumping Between Sections: To quickly jump between sections, click on the section header in the navigation pane. This brings the first card of the selected section into the main editing area.

Using the Search Function

For presentations with extensive content, manually scrolling through cards might not be efficient. Sway's search function can help you locate specific cards quickly:

1. Search Bar: The search bar is located at the top of the navigation pane. Enter keywords or phrases related to the content you're looking for.

2. Search Results: As you type, Sway displays search results, highlighting cards that match your query. Click on a result to navigate directly to the corresponding card.

Previewing Your Sway

Previewing your Sway is an essential step to ensure that your presentation flows smoothly and looks as intended. The navigation pane plays a role in this process as well:

1. Preview Mode: Click on the "Play" button at the top-right corner of the Sway interface to enter preview mode. This allows you to see your Sway as your audience will.

2. Navigating in Preview Mode: Use the navigation arrows or scroll through the preview to experience the flow of your presentation. This helps in identifying any navigation issues or areas that need adjustment.

3. Returning to Edit Mode: Exit preview mode by clicking the "Edit" button. You can then make any necessary changes based on your preview.

Tips for Effective Navigation

To make the most out of the navigation pane and ensure smooth navigation through your Sway cards, consider the following tips:

1. Keep It Organized: Regularly review and organize your cards and sections. An organized Sway is easier to navigate and presents a clearer message to your audience.

2. Use Descriptive Titles: Give each card and section a descriptive title. This makes it easier to identify the content and navigate through the presentation.

3. Regularly Save Your Work: Although Sway automatically saves your changes, it's good practice to manually save your work, especially after significant edits.

4. Practice Your Presentation: Familiarize yourself with the navigation flow by practicing your presentation multiple times. This helps in identifying any areas that need improvement.

By mastering the navigation of Sway cards, you can create more effective and engaging presentations. Efficient navigation allows you to manage your content seamlessly, ensuring that your audience remains engaged and your message is conveyed clearly.

2.3.2 Previewing Your Sway

Previewing your Sway is a crucial step in the content creation process. It allows you to see your presentation as viewers will experience it, ensuring that your layout, transitions, and content flow smoothly. Microsoft Sway offers several features and options for previewing your work, each designed to provide you with a comprehensive view of your project before sharing it with others.

Live Preview Mode

Live Preview mode in Microsoft Sway dynamically updates your presentation as you make changes, giving you an instant preview of how each edit affects the overall look and feel of your Sway. This real-time feedback is invaluable for fine-tuning your design choices and ensuring that your content appears as intended across different devices and screen sizes.

To access Live Preview mode:

1. Navigate to the Design Tab: Click on the Design tab located in the top menu of the Sway interface.

2. Enable Live Preview: Toggle the Live Preview button to turn it on. Once enabled, any changes you make to your Sway will be immediately reflected in the preview pane.

Playback Options

Microsoft Sway allows you to simulate how your presentation will play out to viewers using playback options. This feature is particularly useful for testing interactive elements such as embedded media, navigation buttons, and animations. By simulating the playback, you can ensure that your Sway delivers a seamless and engaging experience for your audience.

To use playback options:

1. Navigate to the Playback Settings: In the Navigation Pane, locate the Playback settings.

2. Adjust Playback Speed: Choose from options such as normal speed, slow motion, or fast forward to observe how transitions and animations appear during playback.

3. Interactive Element Testing: Use playback to interact with embedded media, such as videos and audio files, to verify functionality and playback quality.

Previewing Different Layouts

Microsoft Sway offers various layout options to present your content in different styles, such as vertical or horizontal scrolling, or a mixed layout combining both. Previewing these layouts allows you to see how your content adapts and flows within each design choice, ensuring optimal readability and visual appeal.

To preview different layouts:

1. Select Layout Options: Navigate to the Design tab and choose from the available layout options, such as Vertical, Horizontal, or Slideshow.

2. Navigate Through Layouts: Use the Navigation Pane to switch between different layouts and observe how each one impacts the presentation of your content.

3. Optimizing Content Placement: Adjust the placement of cards and media within each layout to achieve the desired visual hierarchy and storytelling flow.

Responsive Design Preview

One of the key advantages of using Microsoft Sway is its responsive design capabilities, which automatically optimize your presentation for viewing on various devices, including desktops, tablets, and smartphones. Previewing your Sway in responsive design mode allows you to ensure that your content maintains its integrity and readability across different screen sizes and orientations.

To preview responsive design:

1. Toggle Responsive Design Mode: Access the Design tab and toggle the Responsive Design button to activate this mode.

2. View Across Devices: Use the preview pane to simulate how your Sway appears on different devices. Pay attention to font sizes, image resolutions, and layout adjustments made by Sway to accommodate smaller screens.

Accessibility Preview

Accessibility is an important consideration when creating digital content. Microsoft Sway includes built-in accessibility features that allow you to preview your presentation from an accessibility standpoint. This ensures that your content is easily navigable and understandable for users with disabilities, including screen readers and keyboard navigation.

To preview accessibility features:

1. Accessibility Settings: Navigate to the Accessibility settings within the Design tab or Navigation Pane.

2. Verify Accessibility Compliance: Use the preview pane to test how your Sway interacts with assistive technologies. Ensure that all text is properly labeled, images have descriptive alt text, and navigation is intuitive for keyboard users.

Sharing and Preview Links

Before finalizing your Sway and sharing it with others, Microsoft Sway provides options to generate preview links. These links allow you to view and share a read-only version of your presentation without granting full editing access. Preview links are ideal for gathering feedback from collaborators or stakeholders before publishing your Sway publicly.

To generate a preview link:

1. Access Sharing Options: Navigate to the Share tab or sharing settings within the Navigation Pane.

2. Generate Preview Link: Click on the option to create a preview link. Copy and share the generated URL with desired recipients for review and feedback.

Best Practices for Previewing Your Sway

- Regularly Review Changes: Use preview features frequently throughout the creation process to assess the impact of each edit on your overall presentation.

- Test Across Devices: Preview your Sway on different devices and screen sizes to ensure a consistent viewing experience for all users.

- Solicit Feedback: Share preview links with colleagues or peers to gather constructive feedback on your content, layout, and design choices.

CHAPTER III
Creating Your First Sway

3.1 Starting a New Sway

Creating your first Sway can be an exciting experience. Microsoft Sway offers a variety of tools to help you design a professional and engaging presentation. One of the simplest ways to get started is by using a template. Templates provide a pre-designed structure that you can customize according to your needs, saving time and effort while ensuring a polished result. In this section, we will explore how to use a template to create a new Sway.

3.1.1 Using a Template

Templates in Microsoft Sway are a fantastic starting point, especially for beginners. They offer predefined layouts and styles, allowing you to focus more on content creation rather than design. Here's a step-by-step guide on how to use a template in Microsoft Sway:

Step 1: Accessing Templates

1. Login to Sway: Start by logging into your Microsoft account and navigating to the Sway homepage. You can do this by visiting sway.office.com.

2. Create New Sway: Once you're on the Sway dashboard, click on the "Create New" button. This will open a new screen where you can choose to start from scratch or use a template.

3. Browse Templates: Click on the "Start from a template" option. This will open a gallery of available templates, categorized by different themes and purposes such as newsletters, portfolios, reports, and presentations.

Step 2: Choosing the Right Template

1. Template Categories: Browse through the categories to find a template that suits your needs. Templates are organized by use-case scenarios, making it easier to find one that aligns with your project's purpose.

2. Preview Templates: Click on any template thumbnail to preview its layout and design. This will give you an idea of the structure and visual style before you make a selection.

3. Select Template: Once you find a template you like, click on the "Start with this template" button. This will create a new Sway based on the selected template, ready for customization.

Step 3: Customizing the Template

1. Edit Title: The first thing you will see in your new Sway is the title card. Click on it to edit the title of your Sway. This will be the main heading and should reflect the topic of your presentation.

2. Replace Placeholder Content: Templates come with placeholder content that serves as a guide. Click on any text or media card to replace it with your own content. You can add your own text, images, videos, and other media elements.

3. Add New Cards: While templates provide a good structure, you can always add more cards to suit your needs. Click on the "+" button at the bottom of any card to add a new one. You can choose from text, media, and group cards.

Step 4: Adjusting the Layout and Design

1. Design Tab: Switch to the "Design" tab to adjust the overall look of your Sway. Here, you can choose different design styles, change the color scheme, and adjust the layout.

2. Customize Styles: Click on the "Styles" button to explore more customization options. You can adjust the font style, size, and color to match your branding or personal preference.

3. Remix Feature: If you're not satisfied with the current design, use the "Remix" button. This feature automatically applies new design styles to your Sway, giving you different layout options to choose from.

Step 5: Preview and Adjust

1. Preview Your Sway: Before finalizing your Sway, it's important to preview it. Click on the "Play" button to see how your Sway will appear to your audience. This allows you to experience the interactive elements and overall flow.

2. Make Adjustments: Based on the preview, make any necessary adjustments. This could include tweaking the design, rearranging cards, or modifying content to ensure a smooth and engaging presentation.

Step 6: Save and Share

1. Save Your Sway: Sway automatically saves your work, but it's always good to ensure everything is saved correctly. Click on the menu icon and select "Save."

2. Share Your Sway: Once you're satisfied with your Sway, click on the "Share" button to generate a shareable link. You can adjust the sharing settings to control who can view or edit your Sway.

Using a template in Microsoft Sway simplifies the creation process, allowing you to produce professional-looking presentations with ease. Templates provide a solid foundation, enabling you to focus on adding and customizing your content rather than worrying about design. This approach is particularly useful for beginners who might find it challenging to start from a blank canvas.

3.1.2 Starting from Scratch

Starting a new Sway from scratch allows you to have complete control over the design and content of your presentation. This approach is particularly beneficial if you have a specific vision for your Sway that doesn't align with any of the available templates. In this section, we will walk you through the step-by-step process of creating a Sway from scratch, ensuring that you can build a dynamic and engaging presentation from the ground up.

Getting Started

To start a new Sway from scratch, follow these steps:

1. Accessing Sway:

   - Open your web browser and go to the Microsoft Sway website (sway.office.com).

   - Log in with your Microsoft account credentials.

2. Creating a New Sway:

   - Once you're logged in, you'll be directed to the Sway dashboard.

   - Click on the "Create New" button to start a new Sway from scratch.

Building the Foundation

When you start a new Sway from scratch, you'll begin with a blank canvas. This is where you'll build the foundation of your presentation.

1. Title Your Sway:

   - The first thing you'll notice is a prompt to add a title. Click on the title placeholder and enter a title for your Sway. This title will appear at the top of your Sway and serve as the main headline for your presentation.

2. Adding the First Card:

   - After titling your Sway, you'll need to add content cards to build your presentation. Click on the "+" icon to add a new card. You can choose from various types of cards, including text, media, and group cards.

Adding Text Cards

Text cards are fundamental to your Sway as they allow you to add written content. Here's how to effectively use text cards:

1. Inserting Text Cards:

   - Click on the "+" icon and select "Text" from the list of card types.

   - A new text card will appear in the storyline. Click on it to start typing your content.

2. Formatting Text:

   - Sway offers several formatting options to make your text stand out. You can use bold, italic, underline, and bullet points. These options are accessible through the toolbar that appears when you click on the text card.

   - Use headings to structure your content. You can choose from Heading 1, Heading 2, and Heading 3, which helps in creating a hierarchical structure in your presentation.

3. Linking Text:

   - To add hyperlinks, highlight the text you want to link and click on the link icon in the toolbar. Enter the URL and click "Insert." This is useful for directing viewers to additional resources or related content.

Adding Media Cards

Incorporating multimedia elements can make your Sway more engaging. Media cards allow you to add images, videos, audio, and more.

1. Inserting Images:

   - Click on the "+" icon and select "Image" from the media options.

   - You can upload an image from your device, search for one online, or choose from OneDrive.

   - After adding the image, you can resize and reposition it using the controls that appear when you click on the image card.

2. Adding Videos:

   - Click on the "+" icon and select "Video."

   - You can upload a video file, embed a video from YouTube, or record a new video directly within Sway.

   - Embedded videos can be played directly in the presentation, enhancing the interactivity of your Sway.

3. Incorporating Audio:

   - Select the "Audio" option from the media card types.

   - You can upload audio files or record new audio clips. This is particularly useful for narrations or background music.

4. Embedding Content:

   - Sway allows you to embed a wide range of external content, including social media posts, maps, and documents.

- Click on the "+" icon and select "Embed." Paste the embed code of the content you want to include, and it will be integrated into your Sway.

Adding Group Cards

Group cards help you organize multiple pieces of content into a cohesive unit. This is useful for creating sections within your Sway.

1. Creating a Group:

   - Click on the "+" icon and select "Group."

   - Choose the type of group you want to create. Options include stack, comparison, grid, and slideshow.

2. Adding Content to Groups:

   - After selecting a group type, you can start adding content cards to the group.

   - For example, in a stack group, you can add multiple images or text cards that viewers can flip through like a deck of cards.

3. Customizing Groups:

   - Each group type has specific customization options. For instance, in a grid group, you can adjust the number of columns and rows.

   - Use these options to ensure your group is presented in a visually appealing and organized manner.

Customizing Your Sway

Once you've added the basic content, it's time to customize your Sway to match your desired aesthetic and ensure it flows smoothly.

1. Applying Styles:

   - Click on the "Design" tab at the top of the screen.

   - Choose from a variety of design styles to apply to your Sway. Each style offers a different look and feel, from modern and sleek to classic and professional.

- You can also customize individual elements within the design, such as color schemes and fonts, to align with your branding or personal preference.

2. Changing Layouts:

  - Under the "Design" tab, you can also adjust the layout of your Sway.

  - Choose between vertical and horizontal scrolling. Vertical scrolling is more traditional and suited for reports or documents, while horizontal scrolling is great for storytelling and presentations.

  - Experiment with different layouts to see which best suits the structure and content of your Sway.

Previewing and Refining Your Sway

Before finalizing your Sway, it's important to preview it and make any necessary refinements.

1. Previewing Your Sway:

  - Click on the "Play" button at the top of the screen to see how your Sway will appear to viewers.

  - Navigate through your Sway to check for any issues or areas that need improvement.

2. Making Adjustments:

  - Based on your preview, go back to the storyline and make any necessary adjustments.

  - This could include editing text for clarity, repositioning media for better visual flow, or tweaking the design for a more polished look.

3. Finalizing Your Sway:

  - Once you're satisfied with your Sway, ensure all elements are properly aligned and formatted.

  - Double-check all links and embedded content to make sure they are functioning correctly.

Starting a new Sway from scratch gives you the flexibility to create a presentation that is truly unique and tailored to your needs. By following these steps and utilizing the various tools and features available in Sway, you can build an engaging and professional presentation that effectively communicates your message.

3.2 Adding Content to Your Sway

Adding content to your Sway is an essential part of creating a compelling and engaging presentation. Microsoft Sway allows you to incorporate various types of content, including text, images, videos, and embedded elements, to enrich your storytelling. In this section, we will focus on the different types of content cards available in Sway, starting with Text Cards.

3.2.1 Text Cards

Text Cards are the backbone of any Sway presentation. They allow you to add written content, which is crucial for conveying your message, providing explanations, and adding context to your visual elements. In this subsection, we will explore the different aspects of using Text Cards in Sway, including how to add them, format them, and utilize advanced features to make your text more engaging.

Adding Text Cards

To add a Text Card in Sway, follow these steps:

1. Open Your Sway: Start by opening the Sway presentation to which you want to add text.

2. Navigate to the Storyline: Click on the "Storyline" tab if you are not already there. The Storyline is where you manage the sequence of your content.

3. Add a Card: Click the "+" button to add a new card. From the menu that appears, select "Text" to insert a Text Card.

Once the Text Card is added, you can start typing your content. Sway automatically saves your changes, so there's no need to worry about losing your work.

Formatting Text

Formatting text in Sway is straightforward, and it offers several options to make your text stand out. Here are the key formatting features you can use:

1. Basic Formatting: Use the toolbar above the Text Card to apply basic formatting options such as bold, italic, underline, and strikethrough. These options help emphasize important points and improve readability.

2. Headings: Sway allows you to create hierarchical structures within your text by using headings. There are three levels of headings: Heading 1, Heading 2, and Heading 3. To apply a heading, highlight the text you want to format and select the appropriate heading level from the toolbar. Headings are crucial for organizing your content and making it easier for readers to navigate through your Sway.

3. Lists: You can create bulleted or numbered lists to present information in a clear and concise manner. Lists are particularly useful for highlighting key points, steps in a process, or any information that benefits from being broken down into discrete items.

4. Quotes: To emphasize a particular piece of text or to highlight a quote, you can use the "Quote" formatting option. This adds a distinctive style to the text, making it stand out from the rest of the content.

5. Links: Adding hyperlinks to your text is a great way to provide additional information or direct readers to external resources. To add a link, highlight the text you want to link, click the "Link" icon in the toolbar, and enter the URL.

Advanced Text Features

In addition to basic formatting, Sway offers several advanced features to enhance your text content:

1. Text Emphasis: Sway includes a unique "Emphasis" feature that allows you to apply a subtle highlight to text. This is different from bold or italic formatting and is used to draw attention without overwhelming the reader. To apply emphasis, highlight the text and click the "Emphasis" button in the toolbar.

2. Text Backgrounds: To make certain text stand out, you can add a background color to the Text Card. This feature is useful for creating callout boxes or highlighting important sections. To add a background, click on the "Design" tab, select the Text Card, and choose a background color.

3. Text Alignment: You can align your text to the left, center, or right. This is useful for creating a specific layout or design aesthetic. To change the alignment, select the text and click the appropriate alignment button in the toolbar.

4. Combining Text with Media: Sway allows you to combine text with media elements such as images and videos within the same card. This feature is particularly useful for creating multimedia-rich presentations. To combine text with media, simply add the media element to the Text Card and adjust the layout as needed.

Using Text Cards Effectively

While the technical aspects of adding and formatting text in Sway are important, it's equally crucial to consider how you use text to enhance your presentation. Here are some tips for using Text Cards effectively:

1. Be Concise: Sway is designed for visually engaging presentations, so keep your text concise and to the point. Use short paragraphs and bullet points to convey your message clearly.

2. Engage Your Audience: Use engaging language and varied sentence structures to keep your audience interested. Ask questions, use anecdotes, and include calls to action where appropriate.

3. Organize Your Content: Use headings, lists, and other formatting options to organize your content logically. This makes it easier for readers to follow your presentation and find the information they need.

4. Incorporate Visuals: Whenever possible, combine text with visuals to create a more dynamic and engaging presentation. Images, videos, and other media elements can help illustrate your points and make your content more memorable.

5. Edit and Revise: Always review your text for clarity, grammar, and spelling. A well-edited presentation reflects professionalism and ensures that your message is communicated effectively.

Practical Examples

To help you get started with Text Cards, here are some practical examples of how to use them in different scenarios:

1. Business Presentation: In a business presentation, you might use Text Cards to outline key points of a strategy, summarize data, or provide insights. For instance, you could use a

combination of headings, bullet points, and quotes to create a clear and impactful presentation.

2. Educational Content: For educational content, Text Cards can be used to explain concepts, provide step-by-step instructions, or present case studies. You can enhance the text with images, diagrams, and embedded videos to create an engaging learning experience.

3. Personal Project: If you are creating a personal project, such as a travel journal or a family newsletter, Text Cards allow you to narrate your story, describe events, and share experiences. Combine text with photos and maps to create a vivid and personalized presentation.

Conclusion

Text Cards are a fundamental component of any Sway presentation. By mastering the use of Text Cards, you can create engaging, organized, and visually appealing presentations that effectively convey your message. Whether you are creating a business report, educational material, or a personal project, the ability to add, format, and enhance text content in Sway will significantly improve the quality of your presentations. Remember to be concise, engage your audience, organize your content logically, incorporate visuals, and always review your text to ensure clarity and professionalism. With these tips and techniques, you are well on your way to creating compelling Sway presentations using Text Cards.

3.2.2 Media Cards

Media cards in Microsoft Sway are essential for creating dynamic and engaging presentations. They allow you to insert various types of media, such as images, videos, audio, and embedded content, which can significantly enhance the storytelling aspect of your Sway. In this section, we will explore the different types of media cards available, how to add them to your Sway, and tips for maximizing their impact.

Types of Media Cards

1. Image Cards

- Description: Image cards allow you to add pictures to your Sway. Images can be sourced from your device, OneDrive, or the web.

- Usage: Ideal for visual storytelling, creating galleries, or emphasizing points with relevant visuals.

2. Video Cards

- Description: Video cards enable you to insert video content from your device or embed videos from platforms like YouTube.

- Usage: Perfect for demonstrating processes, sharing interviews, or adding multimedia elements to your presentations.

3. Audio Cards

- Description: Audio cards let you add sound clips to your Sway. This can include music, voiceovers, or sound effects.

- Usage: Useful for podcasts, background music, or narration to complement your visual content.

4. Embed Cards

- Description: Embed cards allow you to insert external content such as maps, social media posts, or interactive elements using embed codes.

- Usage: Great for adding interactive maps, live social media feeds, or other web content to your Sway.

Adding Media Cards to Your Sway

1. Adding Image Cards

To add an image card:

- Step 1: Click the "+" button in the Storyline where you want to add the image.

- Step 2: Select "Media" from the list of card types.

- Step 3: Choose "Image" from the options provided.

- Step 4: You can then upload an image from your device, select one from your OneDrive, or search for an image online.

Best Practices for Image Cards:

  - Quality Matters: Use high-resolution images to ensure clarity and professionalism.

  - Relevance: Choose images that are directly related to your content to enhance understanding.

  - Alt Text: Always add alt text for accessibility purposes, describing the content of the image for those using screen readers.

2. Adding Video Cards

To add a video card:

  - Step 1: Click the "+" button in the Storyline where you want to add the video.

  - Step 2: Select "Media" and then "Video" from the options.

  - Step 3: You can either upload a video file from your device or embed a video from platforms like YouTube.

  - Step 4: If embedding, paste the URL of the video in the provided field.

Best Practices for Video Cards:

  - Keep it Short: Aim for concise videos to maintain audience engagement.

  - Subtitles: Include subtitles or captions for accessibility and to cater to a wider audience.

  - High Quality: Ensure the video is of high quality and loads quickly to avoid interruptions.

3. Adding Audio Cards

To add an audio card:

  - Step 1: Click the "+" button in the Storyline where you want to add the audio.

  - Step 2: Select "Media" and then "Audio" from the options.

  - Step 3: Upload your audio file from your device.

Best Practices for Audio Cards:

- Clarity: Ensure the audio is clear and free from background noise.

- Volume: Check the volume levels to ensure they are consistent and not too loud or too soft.

- Context: Use audio that adds value to your content, such as explanations, music that sets the tone, or sound effects that emphasize points.

4. Adding Embed Cards

To add an embed card:

- Step 1: Click the "+" button in the Storyline where you want to add the embedded content.

- Step 2: Select "Media" and then "Embed" from the options.

- Step 3: Paste the embed code into the provided field.

Best Practices for Embed Cards:

- Relevance: Ensure the embedded content is directly related to your presentation.

- Functionality: Test the embedded content to ensure it works correctly within your Sway.

- Interactive Elements: Use embeds for interactive maps, live social media feeds, or other engaging content to enhance the user experience.

Tips for Maximizing the Impact of Media Cards

1. Consistency:

- Maintain a consistent style and theme across all your media cards. This creates a cohesive and professional look.

2. Balance:

- Strike a balance between text and media. Overloading your Sway with too many media elements can be overwhelming. Aim for a harmonious blend.

3. Engagement:

- Use media cards strategically to keep your audience engaged. For example, breaking up long sections of text with relevant images or videos can keep readers interested.

4. Storytelling:

  - Leverage media cards to tell a story. Sequential images, videos, or a combination of media can create a compelling narrative.

5. Accessibility:

  - Ensure all media elements are accessible. Use alt text for images, captions for videos, and clear audio for sound clips.

6. Quality over Quantity:

  - Prioritize high-quality media over quantity. One impactful video or image can be more effective than multiple lower-quality ones.

Examples of Effective Media Card Usage

1. Educational Sway:

  - An educational Sway on environmental science might use image cards to show different ecosystems, video cards to present short documentaries, and embed cards to include interactive maps of wildlife distribution.

2. Business Presentation:

  - A business Sway could include video cards with CEO interviews, image cards of product launches, and embed cards with real-time sales data charts.

3. Personal Project:

  - A personal project Sway, such as a travel journal, might feature image cards of various locations, audio cards with ambient sounds from those places, and embed cards with interactive maps of the travel route.

Conclusion

Media cards are a powerful tool in Microsoft Sway, providing the ability to enrich your presentations with dynamic and engaging content. By understanding the different types of media cards and how to use them effectively, you can create presentations that captivate and inform your audience. Remember to balance media with text, maintain a consistent style, and always consider accessibility to ensure your Sway is both impactful and inclusive. Whether you are creating an educational resource, a business presentation, or a personal project, leveraging media cards will help you communicate your message more effectively and leave a lasting impression on your audience.

3.2.3 Group Cards

Group Cards are a powerful feature in Microsoft Sway that allows you to combine multiple pieces of content into a single, cohesive unit. This feature is particularly useful when you want to present related information together in a visually appealing and organized manner. In this section, we will explore the different types of Group Cards available in Sway, how to create them, and best practices for using them effectively.

Types of Group Cards

Microsoft Sway offers several types of Group Cards, each designed to cater to different presentation needs. These include:

1. Stack Group: Displays content in a stack, allowing users to click through each item.

2. Grid Group: Arranges content in a grid format, making it easy to view multiple items at once.

3. Comparison Group: Allows you to place two pieces of content side by side for comparison.

4. Slideshow Group: Presents content in a slideshow format, ideal for sequential viewing.

5. Automatic Group: Automatically groups related content based on context and layout preferences.

Creating Group Cards

Creating a Group Card in Sway is a straightforward process. Follow these steps to create and customize Group Cards:

Step-by-Step Guide

1. Open Your Sway:

   - Navigate to the Sway you want to edit. If you haven't created one yet, follow the steps in the previous sections to start a new Sway.

2. Access the Group Card Options:

   - In the Storyline pane, click on the "+" button to add a new card.

   - Select "Group" from the dropdown menu to view the different Group Card options.

3. Choose the Group Type:

   - Select the type of Group Card you want to use (Stack, Grid, Comparison, Slideshow, or Automatic).

   - For this example, let's start with a Stack Group.

4. Add Content to the Group:

   - After selecting the Group Card type, you will see a placeholder in your Storyline.

   - Click on the placeholder and start adding content cards within the group by clicking the "+" button and selecting the type of content you want to add (Text, Image, Video, etc.).

5. Customize the Group Card:

   - You can drag and drop to rearrange the order of content within the group.

   - Use the design options to customize the appearance of your Group Card to match your Sway's overall theme.

Example: Creating a Stack Group

Imagine you are creating a Sway to present a project proposal. You want to group together several images, a video, and some text descriptions that outline different aspects of your project.

1. Add a Stack Group:

- Click the "+" button in the Storyline.

- Select "Group" and then choose "Stack".

2. Insert Content into the Stack:

- Click on the Stack Group placeholder.

- Add an Image Card for the project logo.

- Add a Text Card with a brief description of the project.

- Insert a Video Card with a project demo.

- Add more Image Cards showcasing different project features.

3. Arrange and Customize:

- Drag the content cards to arrange them in the desired order.

- Click on each card to customize its appearance (e.g., adding captions to images or adjusting text formatting).

Best Practices for Using Group Cards

To make the most of Group Cards in your Sway, consider the following best practices:

1. Keep Content Related: Group Cards work best when the content within them is closely related. This helps maintain a coherent narrative and enhances the viewer's understanding.

2. Use Descriptive Titles: Each Group Card should have a descriptive title that clearly indicates the content it contains. This helps viewers know what to expect.

3. Balance Visual and Textual Content: Aim for a balance between visual elements (images, videos) and textual content. This keeps your Sway engaging and informative.

4. Leverage Interactive Elements: Group Cards, especially Stack and Slideshow, are inherently interactive. Encourage viewers to click through the content to explore it fully.

5. Maintain Consistency: Ensure that the design and layout of your Group Cards are consistent with the overall theme of your Sway. This creates a professional and polished look.

Examples of Effective Group Card Use

Educational Content

An educator creating a lesson on the solar system could use a Grid Group to present information about each planet. Each cell in the grid could contain an image of the planet, its name, and a brief description. This layout allows students to quickly compare and contrast different planets.

Business Presentation

A business professional could use a Comparison Group to present a SWOT analysis (Strengths, Weaknesses, Opportunities, Threats) of a business strategy. Each side of the comparison could focus on different aspects, making it easy for stakeholders to see the pros and cons at a glance.

Personal Project

Someone documenting a travel experience might use a Slideshow Group to showcase a series of photos from their trip. Each slide could contain a photo and a short description, allowing viewers to click through and experience the journey sequentially.

Advanced Group Card Customizations

For users looking to take their Sway presentations to the next level, there are advanced customization options available:

1. Embedding External Content: You can embed external content such as social media posts, maps, and other interactive elements within your Group Cards.

2. Using Custom CSS: For users with a background in web design, Sway allows the use of custom CSS to further customize the look and feel of your Group Cards.

3. Integrating with Other Microsoft Services: Sway integrates seamlessly with other Microsoft services like OneDrive, SharePoint, and Office 365. You can pull in documents, spreadsheets, and other files directly into your Group Cards.

Conclusion

Group Cards are an essential feature in Microsoft Sway that enhance the way you present and organize content. Whether you're creating educational materials, business presentations, or personal projects, Group Cards provide the flexibility and functionality needed to create engaging and interactive Sways. By understanding the different types of Group Cards and following best practices, you can ensure that your Sway presentations are both visually appealing and highly informative.

Experiment with different Group Card types and customizations to find what works best for your specific needs. With practice and creativity, you'll be able to create professional and impactful presentations using Microsoft Sway.

3.3 Customizing Your Sway

3.3.1 Applying Styles

Customizing your Microsoft Sway presentation allows you to create a visually appealing and engaging experience for your audience. The application of styles is a crucial aspect of this customization process. In this section, we will delve into the methods and best practices for applying styles in Sway to enhance your content's appearance and effectiveness.

Understanding Styles in Sway

Microsoft Sway offers a range of styles that you can apply to your presentation. These styles encompass a variety of elements, including fonts, colors, and layouts. By understanding how to use these styles effectively, you can create a cohesive and professional-looking presentation.

Accessing Style Options

To access the style options in Sway, navigate to the Design tab in the upper menu. Here, you will find several style categories, such as:

- Themes: Predefined sets of colors, fonts, and layouts.

- Color Choices: Options for adjusting the color scheme.

- Font Choices: Options for selecting different font styles.

- Animation: Controls for adding and modifying animation effects.

Each of these categories provides various choices that can be customized further to suit your needs.

Applying Themes

Themes are a great starting point for styling your Sway presentation. They provide a unified look and feel, ensuring consistency across all elements. Here's how to apply a theme:

1. Select a Theme: In the Design tab, scroll through the available themes. Each theme is a combination of colors, fonts, and layouts that work well together.

2. Preview the Theme: Hover over a theme to see a live preview of how it will look in your presentation.

3. Apply the Theme: Click on the theme to apply it to your entire Sway.

Choosing the right theme sets the foundation for the rest of your styling efforts. Ensure the theme aligns with the tone and purpose of your presentation.

Customizing Color Choices

After applying a theme, you can further customize the color scheme to better match your brand or personal preference. To adjust colors:

1. Open the Color Picker: In the Design tab, click on the Colors option.

2. Choose a Palette: Sway offers several predefined color palettes. Select one that complements your content.

3. Custom Colors: If the predefined palettes do not meet your needs, you can create a custom palette. Click on the custom color option and use the color picker to select your desired colors.

Effective use of colors can significantly enhance the visual appeal of your presentation. Consider using a color wheel or other color theory resources to select harmonious color combinations.

Selecting Font Styles

Fonts play a critical role in the readability and aesthetic of your presentation. To change the font styles:

1. Access Font Options: In the Design tab, click on the Fonts option.

2. Choose a Font Pairing: Sway provides several font pairings that include a header font and a body text font. Select a pairing that matches the tone of your presentation.

3. Custom Fonts: If you have specific fonts in mind, you can import them into Sway (subject to availability and compatibility).

When choosing fonts, ensure they are easy to read and appropriate for your audience. Avoid using too many different fonts as this can create a cluttered and unprofessional look.

Adjusting Layouts

Layouts determine the structure and flow of your content. Sway offers flexible layout options that can be tailored to your needs:

1. Layout Options: In the Design tab, select the Layout option.

2. Choose a Layout Style: Sway provides several layout styles such as Vertical, Horizontal, and Grid. Select the one that best suits your content.

3. Customize Layout Elements: Within each layout style, you can adjust specific elements like the arrangement of text and media cards.

Experimenting with different layouts can help you find the most effective way to present your information. Consider the nature of your content and how your audience will interact with it when choosing a layout.

Using the Remix Feature

The Remix feature in Sway is a powerful tool that allows you to quickly apply different styles and see how they affect your presentation. Here's how to use it:

1. Activate Remix: In the Design tab, click on the Remix button.

2. Explore Variations: Sway will automatically apply various style combinations to your presentation. You can cycle through these variations to find one that appeals to you.

3. Apply and Customize: Once you find a variation you like, you can apply it and further customize it as needed.

The Remix feature is particularly useful if you're looking for inspiration or want to explore different style possibilities without manually adjusting each setting.

Advanced Styling Techniques

For users who want to delve deeper into customization, Sway offers advanced styling techniques:

1. Custom CSS: For those familiar with CSS (Cascading Style Sheets), Sway allows you to add custom CSS to further tailor the appearance of your presentation. This feature can be accessed through the settings menu.

2. Embed Interactive Elements: Enhance your Sway by embedding interactive elements like polls, quizzes, and maps. These elements can be styled to match your overall design.

3. Integration with Other Tools: Sway can integrate with other Microsoft tools like Power BI and SharePoint, allowing you to embed dynamic data visualizations and other interactive content.

Best Practices for Applying Styles

To make the most of the styling options in Sway, consider the following best practices:

1. Consistency: Maintain a consistent style throughout your presentation. This includes using the same font styles, color schemes, and layouts.

2. Readability: Ensure your text is easy to read. Avoid using overly decorative fonts and ensure there is sufficient contrast between text and background colors.

3. Visual Hierarchy: Use styling to create a clear visual hierarchy. Headers should stand out from body text, and important information should be highlighted.

4. Simplicity: Less is often more. Avoid overloading your presentation with too many different styles. A clean and simple design is usually more effective.

5. Audience Consideration: Tailor your styling choices to the preferences and expectations of your audience. For example, a corporate presentation might require a more formal style, while a creative portfolio can be more visually expressive.

Conclusion

Applying styles in Microsoft Sway is a crucial step in creating a polished and professional presentation. By understanding and utilizing the various styling options available, you can ensure your content is not only visually appealing but also effectively communicates your message. Whether you are using predefined themes, customizing colors and fonts, adjusting layouts, or using advanced techniques, the key is to maintain a consistent and cohesive look that enhances the overall presentation. With practice and experimentation, you will be able to leverage the full potential of Sway's styling capabilities to create stunning and impactful presentations.

3.3.2 Changing Layouts

One of the key features that sets Microsoft Sway apart from traditional presentation tools is its flexible and dynamic layout options. The layout of your Sway determines how your content is displayed and navigated by viewers. Understanding and utilizing different layout options can greatly enhance the visual appeal and effectiveness of your Sway presentations.

Understanding Layout Options

Microsoft Sway offers several layout options to choose from, each designed to present your content in a unique way. These layouts are categorized into three main types: Vertical, Horizontal, and Slideshow. Each layout type offers different advantages, and the choice of layout depends on the nature of your content and your presentation goals.

1. Vertical Layout: This layout presents content in a continuous vertical scroll. It is ideal for storytelling or narrative-style presentations where the viewer progresses through the content linearly, much like reading a webpage or a blog post. This layout is intuitive and easy to navigate on both desktop and mobile devices.

2. Horizontal Layout: In this layout, content is displayed in a horizontal scroll. This is similar to flipping through pages of a book or a photo album. It is particularly useful for visual-heavy presentations, such as portfolios or image galleries, where the viewer can swipe through images or sections horizontally.

3. Slideshow Layout: This layout mimics a traditional slide presentation where each piece of content is presented one slide at a time. It is effective for structured presentations such

as lectures, business reports, or any scenario where the presenter needs to control the flow of information, one slide at a time.

Choosing the Right Layout

When choosing a layout for your Sway, consider the following factors:

- Content Type: Determine whether your content is primarily text-based, visual, or a mix of both. Text-heavy content may benefit from a vertical layout, while visual content can be showcased effectively in a horizontal or slideshow layout.

- Audience Engagement: Think about how you want your audience to engage with your content. If you want them to scroll through a continuous narrative, a vertical layout is ideal. For more interactive or image-driven content, a horizontal layout might be more engaging.

- Device Compatibility: Consider the devices your audience will use to view your Sway. Vertical layouts are generally more mobile-friendly, while horizontal layouts might work better on larger screens.

How to Change Layouts in Sway

Changing the layout in Microsoft Sway is a straightforward process. Here are the steps to customize your Sway layout:

1. Open Your Sway: Start by opening the Sway you want to edit. You can do this by navigating to your Sway dashboard and selecting the appropriate Sway from your list of projects.

2. Access Design Options: Click on the "Design" tab located at the top of the Sway interface. This tab contains various options for customizing the look and feel of your Sway.

3. Select a Layout: Within the Design tab, you will see the "Layout" section. Here, you can choose from the available layout options: Vertical, Horizontal, and Slideshow. Click on the layout you want to apply to your Sway.

4. Preview Changes: After selecting a layout, use the "Preview" button to see how your content will appear in the new layout. This allows you to make sure the chosen layout enhances the presentation of your content.

5. Adjust Content if Necessary: Depending on the layout you choose, you might need to adjust the placement of certain elements or reformat text to ensure optimal viewing. For example, in a horizontal layout, you might want to group related images or text blocks together.

6. Save Your Changes: Once you are satisfied with the layout, make sure to save your changes. Your Sway will automatically update with the new layout settings.

Customizing Layout Elements

Beyond simply choosing a layout, Microsoft Sway allows for further customization of how individual elements are displayed within that layout. Here are some tips for fine-tuning your Sway's layout:

- Grouping Content: Use Group Cards to organize related content together. Grouping can enhance the visual flow and make your Sway more cohesive. For example, you can group a series of images into a gallery or combine text and media into a stack.

- Emphasizing Key Points: Highlight important content by using emphasis options. In the storyline, you can mark certain cards as "Emphasized" to make them stand out more prominently in the layout. This is useful for drawing attention to key messages or critical visuals.

- Using Sections: Divide your Sway into sections to create a logical structure. Sections act like chapters in a book, allowing viewers to navigate through your content easily. This is particularly helpful in long Sways where organization is crucial.

- Adjusting Visual Styles: Within each layout, you can further customize the visual style of your content. Use the "Styles" option in the Design tab to apply different themes and color schemes. Experiment with various styles to find one that complements your content and enhances readability.

Advanced Layout Techniques

For users who want to delve deeper into customizing their Sway, here are some advanced techniques:

- Embedding Interactive Content: Enhance your Sway by embedding interactive elements such as maps, videos, and social media posts. These elements can be integrated seamlessly into any layout and add a dynamic aspect to your presentation.

- Utilizing the Remix Feature: The Remix feature allows you to automatically apply a new design to your Sway. If you're unsure about which layout or style to choose, use Remix to explore different possibilities. You can keep remixing until you find a design that suits your needs.

- Customizing with CSS: For users with coding knowledge, Sway offers the option to customize styles using CSS. This provides greater control over the appearance of your Sway, allowing for precise adjustments to fonts, colors, and spacing.

Best Practices for Effective Layouts

To make the most out of Microsoft Sway's layout options, consider these best practices:

- Maintain Consistency: Ensure that your layout choices are consistent throughout your Sway. Consistency in design elements such as fonts, colors, and spacing helps create a professional and polished look.

- Prioritize Readability: No matter which layout you choose, prioritize readability. Avoid cluttering your Sway with too much information or overly complex designs. Use whitespace effectively to give your content room to breathe.

- Focus on Engagement: Design your layout with audience engagement in mind. Use interactive elements, engaging visuals, and concise text to keep viewers interested. The layout should facilitate a smooth and enjoyable viewing experience.

- Test on Multiple Devices: Preview your Sway on different devices to ensure that the layout is responsive and looks good on all screen sizes. This step is crucial for reaching a broader audience and ensuring accessibility.

Conclusion

Changing layouts in Microsoft Sway is a powerful way to enhance your presentations and make your content more engaging. By understanding the different layout options and how to customize them, you can create visually appealing and effective Sways that captivate your audience. Remember to experiment with various layouts, utilize advanced customization techniques, and follow best practices to achieve the best results. With these tools and knowledge, you're well on your way to becoming a Microsoft Sway expert.

CHAPTER IV
Working with Text and Media

4.1 Adding and Formatting Text

4.1.1 Text Basics

Text is a fundamental element of any presentation or digital storytelling project. In Microsoft Sway, adding and formatting text is straightforward, yet the platform offers a range of options that can enhance your content's readability and visual appeal. This section will guide you through the basics of adding and formatting text in Sway.

Understanding Text Cards

In Sway, text is added using "Text Cards." These cards function as containers for your textual content and can be easily manipulated to fit your design needs. There are several types of text cards available:

- Title Card: Used for headings and titles.

- Heading Card: Ideal for subheadings within your Sway.

- Text Card: Used for regular body text.

Each of these cards can be added to your storyline and customized individually.

Adding a Text Card

To add a text card to your Sway:

1. Open Your Sway: Navigate to the Sway you are working on or create a new Sway.

2. Access the Storyline: Click on the "Storyline" tab to view the sequence of your cards.

3. Add a Text Card: Click on the plus (+) button in the place where you want to add text. Select "Text" from the dropdown menu.

You can now start typing directly into the text card that appears. If you want to add a title or heading, select the appropriate card type from the options provided.

Basic Text Entry

Entering text in Sway is as simple as clicking on a text card and typing your content. Here are some tips for basic text entry:

- Click and Type: Click on the text area of the card and start typing.

- Auto-Save: Sway automatically saves your work, so you don't need to worry about losing your text.

- Drag and Drop: You can drag text cards to rearrange the order of your content in the storyline.

Formatting Options

Once you have added text to a card, you can format it to enhance its appearance and readability. Basic formatting options include:

- Bold and Italic: Highlight the text you want to format, and click the "B" button for bold or the "I" button for italic.

- Bulleted and Numbered Lists: Click the bullet or number icon to create lists. Lists help break up text and make it more digestible.

- Hyperlinks: Highlight the text you want to turn into a link, click the link icon, and enter the URL.

Advanced Text Formatting

For more advanced text formatting, Sway provides additional tools:

- Text Alignment: Choose to align your text left, center, or right to match your design preferences.

- Emphasis: Use the emphasis options to draw attention to important sections of your text.

- Highlighting: Apply background color to your text to make it stand out.

Text Styles and Themes

Text styles and themes in Sway can significantly affect the presentation of your text. You can choose from a variety of predefined styles that ensure consistency and visual appeal across your Sway. Here's how to apply text styles:

1. Select a Theme: Go to the "Design" tab and choose a theme that fits your presentation's tone.

2. Apply Styles: Each theme comes with predefined text styles that you can apply to your text cards. These styles include font types, sizes, and colors.

Practical Examples

Let's consider some practical examples of how to use text effectively in Sway:

- Creating a Title Page: Start with a Title Card and type the title of your presentation. Use bold and large font sizes to make it stand out.

- Adding Sections: Use Heading Cards to define different sections of your content. This helps in organizing your Sway and guiding the reader through your narrative.

- Detailed Descriptions: Use Text Cards for paragraphs and detailed descriptions. Break up long paragraphs into shorter ones for better readability.

Best Practices for Text Usage

To make the most out of text in your Sway, consider the following best practices:

- Concise Writing: Keep your text concise and to the point. Sway is designed for visual storytelling, so avoid lengthy blocks of text.

- Use Visuals: Complement your text with images, videos, and other media to create a more engaging presentation.

- Consistent Formatting: Maintain consistent formatting throughout your Sway to provide a cohesive look and feel.

- Readable Fonts: Choose readable fonts and appropriate sizes to ensure your text is easily legible on different devices.

Accessibility Considerations

When adding text to your Sway, it's important to consider accessibility to ensure that all users, including those with disabilities, can access your content. Here are some tips:

- Alt Text for Images: When you add images alongside your text, always include alt text descriptions.

- Contrast: Ensure there is sufficient contrast between your text and background colors.

- Readable Fonts: Use fonts that are easy to read and avoid overly decorative styles.

Troubleshooting Text Issues

While working with text in Sway, you might encounter some common issues. Here are a few troubleshooting tips:

- Text Not Appearing Correctly: Ensure you are using supported fonts and that your text cards are properly formatted.

- Alignment Issues: Double-check the alignment settings and adjust as necessary.

- Hyperlinks Not Working: Verify that the URLs are correct and that the hyperlink is applied properly.

Conclusion

Mastering text basics in Microsoft Sway is essential for creating compelling and effective presentations. By understanding how to add, format, and customize text, you can significantly enhance the visual appeal and readability of your content. Whether you are creating a simple report or an elaborate digital story, the text tools in Sway offer the flexibility and power you need to bring your ideas to life.

In the next section, we will delve deeper into formatting options and advanced techniques to further refine your text and make your Sway presentations truly stand out.

4.1.2 Formatting Options

Microsoft Sway offers a range of formatting options that allow users to customize their text, making their content visually appealing and easy to read. In this section, we will explore various formatting tools available in Sway and how to use them effectively.

Basic Formatting

The basic formatting options in Microsoft Sway include bold, italic, underline, and text alignment. These tools are essential for emphasizing key points and organizing text for better readability.

Bold, Italic, and Underline

- Bold: To make text bold, select the text you want to emphasize and click the bold icon (B) in the toolbar or use the keyboard shortcut `Ctrl + B` (Windows) or `Command + B` (Mac). Bold text is useful for highlighting important information or headings.

- Italic: Italicizing text can be achieved by selecting the text and clicking the italic icon (I) or using the keyboard shortcut `Ctrl + I` (Windows) or `Command + I` (Mac). Italic text is often used for emphasis, quotes, or titles of works.

- Underline: To underline text, select it and click the underline icon (U) or use the keyboard shortcut `Ctrl + U` (Windows) or `Command + U` (Mac). Underlined text can be used for emphasis or hyperlinks.

Text Alignment

Sway allows you to align your text to the left, center, or right. Text alignment is crucial for creating a structured and visually balanced presentation.

- Left Alignment: This is the default setting. To left-align your text, select the text and click the left alignment icon in the toolbar.

- Center Alignment: Center-aligned text is often used for titles or headings. To center-align your text, select the text and click the center alignment icon.

- Right Alignment: Right-aligned text can be used for captions or specific design purposes. To right-align your text, select the text and click the right alignment icon.

Advanced Formatting

Advanced formatting options in Sway provide more ways to customize your text, including bullet points, numbered lists, quotes, and text size adjustments.

Bullet Points and Numbered Lists

- Bullet Points: To create a bulleted list, select the text you want to format and click the bullet points icon in the toolbar. Bullet points are ideal for listing items or key points.

- Numbered Lists: Numbered lists can be created by selecting the text and clicking the numbered list icon. Numbered lists are useful for steps or sequences.

Quotes

Quotes can be highlighted in Sway using the quote formatting option. This is particularly useful for emphasizing important statements or citing sources.

- To format text as a quote, select the text and click the quote icon in the toolbar. The text will be indented and styled differently to stand out from the main content.

Text Size Adjustments

Adjusting the size of your text can help differentiate between headings, subheadings, and body text. Sway offers options to increase or decrease text size.

- Headings: To create a heading, select the text and choose a larger text size from the toolbar. Headings are typically used for section titles and should be visually distinct from body text.

- Subheadings: Subheadings can be created by selecting the text and choosing a slightly smaller text size than the main headings. Subheadings help organize content within a section.

- Body Text: The default text size is usually suitable for body text. However, you can adjust it as needed for readability.

Customizing Text Color

Microsoft Sway allows users to change the color of their text to match the theme or highlight specific sections. Customizing text color can enhance the visual appeal of your presentation.

- Changing Text Color: To change the color of your text, select the text and click the color icon in the toolbar. Choose from the available colors or customize your own. Ensure that the chosen color contrasts well with the background for readability.

Hyperlinks

Adding hyperlinks to your text can provide additional resources or direct readers to related content. Sway makes it easy to insert hyperlinks.

- Inserting a Hyperlink: To insert a hyperlink, select the text you want to link, click the link icon in the toolbar, and enter the URL. Hyperlinked text will be underlined and usually change color to indicate its clickable nature.

Using Emphasis and Accents

Sway provides options to emphasize text using different styles and accents. These options can make your content more engaging.

- Emphasis: Emphasizing text can be done by selecting the text and choosing an emphasis style from the toolbar. Emphasis styles may include bold, italics, or color changes.

- Accents: Accents can be added to text to draw attention to specific words or phrases. Select the text and choose an accent style from the toolbar. This might include highlights or unique fonts.

Combining Formatting Options

Combining various formatting options can create a well-structured and visually appealing presentation. Here are some tips for effectively combining formatting options in Sway:

- Headings and Subheadings: Use bold and larger text sizes for headings and subheadings. This creates a clear hierarchy and helps readers navigate through the content.

- Lists and Bullet Points: Combine bullet points with bold text for key points. This makes the information stand out and easy to scan.

- Quotes and Italics: Use the quote format for important statements and italicize the text for additional emphasis. This makes quotes easily identifiable.

- Text Color and Links: Change the color of hyperlinked text to match the theme of your presentation. This ensures that links are noticeable without disrupting the overall design.

Accessibility Considerations

When formatting text in Sway, it's important to consider accessibility to ensure that all readers can easily engage with your content. Here are some accessibility tips:

- Contrast: Ensure that there is sufficient contrast between the text color and the background. High contrast makes text easier to read for individuals with visual impairments.

- Font Size: Use an appropriate font size for readability. Avoid using excessively small text, especially for body content.

- Alternative Text: When using hyperlinks, provide descriptive alternative text. Instead of "click here," use descriptive text like "learn more about formatting options."

- Consistent Formatting: Maintain consistent formatting throughout your presentation. Consistency helps readers follow the content more easily and reduces cognitive load.

Practical Examples

To illustrate the effective use of formatting options, here are some practical examples:

Example 1: Business Report

- Heading: Bold, large text size

- Subheading: Slightly smaller text size, bold

- Body Text: Default text size

- Bullet Points: Bold key points

- Quotes: Italicized and formatted as quotes

- Hyperlinks: Colored to match the theme

Example 2: Educational Presentation

- Title Slide: Center-aligned, large text size, bold

- Section Headings: Bold, large text size

- Subsections: Italicized subheadings

- Body Text: Standard text size, with key terms bolded

- Lists: Numbered lists for steps, bullet points for lists

- Hyperlinks: Descriptive alternative text

Example 3: Personal Blog Post

- Title: Bold, large text size, centered

- Introduction: Italicized

- Body Text: Standard text size, with occasional bold for emphasis

- Quotes: Indented, italicized, and formatted as quotes

- Hyperlinks: Underlined and colored

Troubleshooting Common Formatting Issues

While formatting text in Sway is generally straightforward, you may encounter some common issues. Here are solutions to common formatting problems:

- Text Not Formatting as Expected: Ensure that the text is properly selected before applying formatting. If the issue persists, try retyping the text and applying the formatting again.

- Inconsistent Formatting: If formatting appears inconsistent, check for conflicting styles. Clear formatting and reapply the desired style to ensure consistency.

- Hyperlinks Not Working: Double-check the URL for accuracy. Ensure that the hyperlink is applied correctly by selecting the text and clicking the link icon.

- Color Contrast Issues: If text color blends with the background, choose a higher contrast color. Use online tools to check color contrast ratios for accessibility.

Best Practices for Text Formatting

To ensure that your text formatting enhances your presentation, consider these best practices:

- Clarity and Readability: Prioritize readability by using clear fonts, appropriate sizes, and high contrast colors. Avoid overly decorative fonts that may be hard to read.

- Consistent Style: Maintain a consistent style for headings, subheadings, and body text. This helps create a cohesive and professional look.

- Balanced Design: Balance text with other elements such as images and videos. Avoid text-heavy slides that can overwhelm readers.

- Highlight Key Points: Use formatting options like bold, italics, and bullet points to highlight key points. This makes important information stand out.

- Review and Revise: Regularly review your presentation for formatting consistency and readability. Make necessary adjustments to improve the overall quality.

Conclusion

Formatting options in Microsoft Sway provide powerful tools to enhance the visual appeal and readability of your presentations. By mastering these options, you can create professional, engaging, and accessible content. Whether you are preparing a business report, educational presentation, or personal project, effective text formatting will help you communicate your message clearly and effectively. As you explore and experiment with Sway's formatting features, remember to consider your audience and purpose, ensuring that your presentation is both visually appealing and easy to understand.

4.2 Inserting Images and Videos

4.2.1 Uploading Your Media

In Microsoft Sway, incorporating media elements such as images and videos can significantly enhance the visual appeal and engagement level of your presentations. The ability to upload your media directly into Sway allows you to personalize and customize your content, making it more relevant and impactful for your audience. In this section, we will delve into the step-by-step process of uploading your media, including images and videos, ensuring you can effectively utilize these tools in your Sway presentations.

Step 1: Accessing the Media Upload Options

To begin uploading your media in Sway, you need to access the media upload options. This can be done by navigating to the Storyline tab where you create and edit your Sway. Here, you'll find options to add different types of content.

1. Navigate to the Storyline Tab: Open your Sway and go to the Storyline tab. This is where you will add and organize your content.

2. Select the Card Type: Click on the plus (+) button to add a new card. From the dropdown menu, you can choose different types of cards. To upload images or videos, you will typically use the "Image" or "Video" card options.

Step 2: Uploading Images

Images are a powerful way to convey messages and add visual interest to your Sway. Here's how you can upload your images:

1. Add an Image Card: Click on the plus (+) button and select "Image" from the card options. This will add an image card to your Storyline.

2. Upload Your Image: Click on the "Add an image" option within the card. This will open a dialogue box where you can choose to upload an image from your device.

- From Your Device: Select "Upload" and browse through your computer files to choose the image you want to upload. Once you find the image, click "Open" to upload it to your Sway.

- From OneDrive: If your images are stored in OneDrive, you can select "OneDrive" to access your cloud storage and choose the image you want to use.

Step 3: Uploading Videos

Videos can bring your Sway presentations to life, providing dynamic and engaging content. Here's how to upload videos:

1. Add a Video Card: Click on the plus (+) button and select "Video" from the card options. This will add a video card to your Storyline.

2. Upload Your Video: Click on the "Add a video" option within the card. Similar to images, this will open a dialogue box where you can choose to upload a video from your device.

- From Your Device: Select "Upload" and browse through your computer files to choose the video you want to upload. Click "Open" to upload it to your Sway.

- From OneDrive: If your videos are stored in OneDrive, you can select "OneDrive" to access your cloud storage and choose the video you want to use.

Step 4: Using Drag and Drop

Sway also supports drag-and-drop functionality, making it even easier to upload media. Here's how:

1. Select Your Media: Open the folder on your computer where your image or video is stored.

2. Drag and Drop: Click and hold the image or video file, drag it over to the Sway window, and drop it into the desired position within the Storyline. Sway will automatically create the appropriate card type and upload your media.

Step 5: Managing Your Uploaded Media

Once your media is uploaded, you may need to manage or edit it to fit your presentation needs. Here are some tips:

1. Resizing and Cropping Images: Click on the uploaded image to access editing options. You can resize or crop the image to better fit the design and layout of your Sway.

2. Trimming Videos: For videos, Sway offers basic trimming options. Click on the uploaded video to access the trim tool, allowing you to cut the video to the desired length.

3. Reordering Media Cards: You can easily change the order of your media cards by dragging and dropping them within the Storyline. This helps in organizing your content flow effectively.

Step 6: Adding Captions and Alt Text

To make your Sway more accessible and informative, you should consider adding captions and alternative text (alt text) to your images and videos.

1. Adding Captions: Click on the image or video card and find the option to add a caption. Write a brief description or context for the media, which will be displayed below it in your Sway.

2. Adding Alt Text: Alt text is important for accessibility, helping screen readers describe the content to visually impaired users. Click on the image or video, select the "Alt Text" option, and enter a descriptive text that explains what the media depicts.

Step 7: Optimizing Media for Performance

Large media files can affect the loading time and performance of your Sway. Here's how to optimize your media:

1. Compress Images: Use image compression tools to reduce the file size of your images without compromising quality. Smaller file sizes will load faster and improve the overall performance of your Sway.

2. Optimize Videos: Consider using video compression tools or choosing a lower resolution to ensure your videos load quickly and play smoothly.

Step 8: Using Media from Online Sources

In addition to uploading your media, Sway allows you to insert media from various online sources. This can save you time and provide access to a wider range of content.

1. Online Images: When adding an image card, select the "Suggested" option to browse and insert images from Bing search, OneDrive, Flickr, and more.

2. Online Videos: For video cards, you can embed videos from YouTube, Vimeo, and other online platforms by selecting the "Suggested" option and searching for the desired video.

Step 9: Ensuring Media Compliance

When using media in your Sway, it's important to ensure that you have the right to use the content. Here are some best practices:

1. Use Licensed Media: Ensure that any media you upload or use from online sources is properly licensed for your intended use. Avoid using copyrighted material without permission.

2. Cite Sources: When using media from online sources, provide proper attribution and citations as required. This not only respects the content creators but also maintains the integrity of your Sway.

Step 10: Testing Your Sway

After uploading and organizing your media, it's crucial to test your Sway to ensure everything displays and functions correctly.

1. Preview Mode: Use the preview mode in Sway to see how your presentation will look to your audience. Check that all images and videos are correctly uploaded and displayed.

2. Check Links and Embeds: Ensure that any embedded content, such as videos from online sources, works properly and links are functional.

3. Cross-Device Testing: Test your Sway on different devices (desktop, tablet, mobile) to ensure it looks and performs well across all platforms.

Conclusion

Uploading your own media to Microsoft Sway allows you to create personalized, engaging, and dynamic presentations. By following the steps outlined in this section, you can confidently add images and videos to your Sway, enhancing the overall impact of your content. Remember to manage your media effectively, optimize for performance, and ensure compliance with usage rights to create professional and compelling Sway presentations.

4.2.2 Searching for Online Media

One of the key features that sets Microsoft Sway apart from other presentation tools is its seamless integration with various online media sources. This capability allows users to enrich their Sway presentations with diverse content, ranging from images and videos to social media posts and maps. In this section, we will explore how to effectively search for and incorporate online media into your Sway projects.

Understanding Online Media Integration

Microsoft Sway provides built-in functionality to search for and embed media from multiple online sources directly within the application. This integration saves time and effort, eliminating the need to switch between different apps or browser tabs to find the content you need. Whether you're looking for royalty-free images, informative videos, or engaging social media posts, Sway makes it easy to add these elements to your presentation.

Accessing the Online Media Search Feature

To begin searching for online media, you need to access the appropriate feature within Sway. Follow these steps:

1. Open Your Sway Project: Start by opening the Sway project where you want to insert the online media.

2. Navigate to the Insert Tab: On the top menu, click on the "Insert" tab. This will open a panel on the right side of the screen with various options for adding content to your Sway.

3. Select an Online Source: In the "Insert" panel, you will see a list of online sources such as Bing Images, YouTube, and more. Click on the source you wish to use for your search.

Searching for Images Online

Images are a vital component of any presentation, helping to convey messages visually and engage the audience. Here's how you can search for and insert images from online sources:

1. Choose Bing Images: In the "Insert" panel, click on "Bing Images." This will open a search bar where you can enter keywords related to the images you need.

2. Enter Search Keywords: Type in the keywords that describe the image you are looking for. For instance, if you're creating a presentation about digital marketing, you might enter "digital marketing" or "online advertising."

3. Filter Search Results: Bing Images offers several filters to help you narrow down your search results. You can filter by image size, layout, color, and even license type to ensure you are using images that are free for public use.

4. Preview and Select Images: Browse through the search results and click on any image to preview it. Once you find an image that fits your needs, click on it to insert it into your Sway.

Searching for Videos Online

Videos can enhance your Sway presentation by providing dynamic content that can explain complex ideas, showcase products, or engage your audience with visual storytelling. To search for and insert videos, follow these steps:

1. Choose YouTube: In the "Insert" panel, click on "YouTube." This will open a search bar for finding YouTube videos.

2. Enter Search Keywords: Type in the keywords related to the video content you are seeking. For example, if you're looking for tutorials on using Sway, you might enter "Microsoft Sway tutorial."

3. Filter Search Results: YouTube provides filters to refine your search results. You can filter by upload date, video duration, and more to find the most relevant videos.

4. Preview and Select Videos: Browse through the search results and click on any video to preview it. Once you find a suitable video, click on it to insert it into your Sway.

Using Other Online Media Sources

In addition to Bing Images and YouTube, Microsoft Sway allows you to search for and insert content from various other online sources. These include:

- Flickr: A popular photo-sharing platform where you can find high-quality images shared by photographers worldwide.

- Pickit: A curated library of royalty-free images that are safe to use in your presentations.

- Twitter: You can embed tweets directly into your Sway to provide real-time updates or showcase social media engagement.

- OneDrive and Facebook: If you have images or videos stored on OneDrive or shared on Facebook, you can easily insert them into your Sway by connecting your accounts.

Best Practices for Searching Online Media

To make the most of the online media search feature in Microsoft Sway, consider the following best practices:

1. Use Specific Keywords: When searching for images or videos, use specific and relevant keywords to find the most accurate results. Broad or generic terms may yield too many irrelevant results.

2. Check Licenses: Ensure that the media you select is free to use, especially for commercial presentations. Use the license filter to find images labeled for reuse.

3. Maintain Consistency: Aim for a consistent style and quality across all the media you insert. This helps create a cohesive and professional-looking presentation.

4. Optimize File Sizes: While Sway handles most media efficiently, it's still a good practice to use optimized file sizes to ensure smooth performance, especially when embedding videos.

5. Consider Accessibility: Include alt text for images and captions for videos to make your Sway accessible to all users, including those with disabilities.

Example: Incorporating Online Media into a Marketing Presentation

Let's walk through a practical example of how to use the online media search feature to enhance a marketing presentation in Sway.

1. Opening the Project: Begin by opening your marketing presentation in Sway.

2. Inserting a Relevant Image: Click on the "Insert" tab, select "Bing Images," and enter "digital marketing strategy." Filter the results to show high-resolution images that are free for public use. Choose an image that best represents your topic and insert it into the introduction section.

3. Adding an Informative Video: Next, click on "YouTube" in the "Insert" panel and search for "digital marketing trends 2024." Filter the results to find the most recent and relevant videos. Preview a few options and select a video that provides valuable insights into current marketing trends. Insert the video into the section discussing future strategies.

4. Embedding a Tweet: To showcase social media engagement, select "Twitter" in the "Insert" panel. Search for tweets using hashtags like DigitalMarketing or MarketingTrends. Find a tweet from a reputable source discussing recent marketing developments and embed it into your Sway.

5. Reviewing and Finalizing: Review your presentation to ensure all media elements are well-integrated and relevant to your content. Make adjustments as needed to maintain a smooth and engaging flow.

Troubleshooting Common Issues

While searching for and inserting online media is generally straightforward, you might encounter some common issues. Here's how to address them:

1. Slow Loading Times: If images or videos take a long time to load, ensure you have a stable internet connection. Large file sizes can also cause delays, so consider using optimized media.

2. Unavailable Content: Sometimes, the media you want to use may no longer be available online. In such cases, try finding alternative sources or similar content.

3. Embedding Errors: If a tweet or video fails to embed properly, check that the URL is correct and that the content is publicly accessible. Private or restricted content cannot be embedded.

Conclusion

Searching for and incorporating online media into your Microsoft Sway presentations can significantly enhance the visual appeal and engagement of your content. By following the steps and best practices outlined in this section, you can effectively utilize images, videos, and other online resources to create dynamic and interactive presentations. Remember to always check the licensing of the media you use and maintain a consistent and professional look throughout your Sway project. With these tools and techniques at your disposal, you are well on your way to mastering the art of creating compelling presentations with Microsoft Sway.

4.3 Embedding Content

4.3.1 Embedding Maps

WelcomeSure, here is the detailed content for section 4.3.1 "Embedding Maps" in the book "Microsoft Sway: The Complete Tutorial for Beginners."

4.3 Embedding Content

Embedding content into your Sway presentation can add a level of interactivity and engagement that static text and images can't match. It allows you to pull in dynamic elements from the web and integrate them seamlessly into your Sway. One of the most useful types of embedded content is maps. Embedding maps can be particularly useful for presentations that require geographic context, such as travel guides, business reports, educational projects, and event planning.

4.3.1 Embedding Maps

Embedding maps in Microsoft Sway enhances your presentations by providing geographical context and interactive navigation. Whether you're showing locations for a travel itinerary, illustrating market regions for a business report, or pinpointing historical sites for an educational project, maps can significantly enhance the viewer's understanding and engagement. This section will guide you through the steps of embedding maps into your Sway, including different methods for adding maps, customizing the appearance, and utilizing interactive features.

Why Use Embedded Maps?

Before diving into the technical steps, let's discuss why embedded maps are valuable:

- Visual Context: Maps provide a visual reference that can make it easier to understand geographic relationships and locations.

- Interactivity: Interactive maps allow viewers to zoom in and out, explore different areas, and gain a deeper understanding of the presented information.

- Engagement: Interactive elements like maps can make your presentation more engaging and dynamic, keeping your audience interested.

Types of Maps You Can Embed

Microsoft Sway supports embedding maps from various sources, including:

- Bing Maps: Microsoft's own mapping service, which integrates seamlessly with Sway.

- Google Maps: A widely-used mapping service that provides extensive geographic data and customization options.

- Other Mapping Services: Many other online mapping services and tools offer embeddable maps, which can also be used in Sway.

How to Embed Bing Maps

Step-by-Step Guide

1. Open Your Sway: Start by opening the Sway in which you want to embed the map. Navigate to the section where you want to insert the map.

2. Insert a New Card: Click on the "+" button to add a new card. Select "Embed" from the available options. This will create an embed card where you can place your map.

3. Access Bing Maps: Open a new browser tab and go to [Bing Maps](https://www.bing.com/maps). Search for the location you want to embed.

4. Get the Embed Code: Once you've found the location, click on the "Share" button (usually represented by an arrow icon) and select "Embed a map." Customize the map view, such as the zoom level and map type (road, aerial, etc.), then copy the embed code provided.

5. Paste the Embed Code in Sway: Go back to your Sway and paste the embed code into the Embed card. Click "Preview" to see how the map looks in your Sway. Adjust the map view if necessary.

Customizing Your Map

Bing Maps allows you to customize the appearance and functionality of the map before embedding it. You can:

- Adjust the Zoom Level: Set the zoom level to show a broader view or a close-up of the location.

- Select the Map Type: Choose between road view, aerial view, and other map types to suit your presentation needs.

- Add Landmarks: Highlight specific points of interest or landmarks on the map to make it more informative.

How to Embed Google Maps

Step-by-Step Guide

1. Open Your Sway: As with Bing Maps, start by opening your Sway and navigating to the section where you want to add the map.

2. Insert a New Card: Click on the "+" button to add a new card and select "Embed" from the options.

3. Access Google Maps: In a new browser tab, go to [Google Maps](https://maps.google.com). Search for the desired location.

4. Get the Embed Code: Click on the "Share" button (usually represented by a chain link icon) and select "Embed a map." Customize the map view, then copy the HTML embed code.

5. Paste the Embed Code in Sway: Return to Sway and paste the embed code into the Embed card. Click "Preview" to check the map's appearance and functionality.

Customizing Your Map

Google Maps offers extensive customization options before generating the embed code. You can:

- Set the Zoom Level: Adjust how zoomed-in or zoomed-out the map should appear.

- Map Type: Choose between map view, satellite view, terrain, and more.

- Directions and Routes: Embed maps with directions and routes if your presentation involves travel or logistics.

Adding Interactive Features to Your Maps

One of the major advantages of embedding maps is the interactivity they offer. Here are some ways to leverage these features:

- Zoom and Pan: Viewers can zoom in and out and pan across the map to explore different areas.

- Clickable Points: Embedded maps from services like Google Maps can include clickable points that provide additional information about specific locations.

- Street View: For supported areas, viewers can switch to street view for a real-world look at the location.

Troubleshooting Embedded Maps

While embedding maps is generally straightforward, you may encounter some issues. Here are common problems and their solutions:

- Map Not Displaying: Ensure that the embed code is correctly copied and pasted. Double-check that the map service's embed feature is working.

- Incorrect Location: Verify that you've selected the correct location before copying the embed code. You may need to adjust the map view.

- Map Not Interactive: Some services may limit interactivity for embedded maps. Ensure you're using an embed code that supports the desired level of interactivity.

Practical Use Cases for Embedded Maps

Travel Guides

If you're creating a travel guide, embedding maps can help readers visualize the destinations you're discussing. You can:

- Highlight Tourist Attractions: Embed maps showing the locations of must-visit sites.

- Plot Travel Routes: Show the best routes between different locations, including driving, walking, or public transportation options.

Business Reports

For business presentations, maps can be used to:

- Illustrate Market Regions: Show geographical regions where your company operates or where market research was conducted.

- Visualize Sales Data: Combine maps with data visualizations to display sales performance across different regions.

Educational Projects

Teachers and students can use embedded maps to:

- Explore Historical Events: Show the locations of significant historical events or timelines.

- Geographical Studies: Illustrate geographical features or demographic data for educational purposes.

Conclusion

Embedding maps in your Sway presentations is a powerful way to enhance your content, providing visual and interactive elements that can help engage your audience and convey information more effectively. Whether you're using Bing Maps, Google Maps, or another mapping service, the process is straightforward and customizable to meet your needs. By following the steps outlined in this section, you can easily embed maps into your Sway and take advantage of the rich, interactive features they offer.

4.3.2 Embedding Social Media Posts

Embedding social media posts into your Sway presentations can significantly enhance the interactivity and engagement of your content. Social media posts can provide real-time information, showcase user-generated content, and add a dynamic layer to your presentation. This section will guide you through the steps and best practices for embedding social media posts from various platforms, such as Twitter, Facebook, Instagram, and LinkedIn, into your Sway.

Why Embed Social Media Posts?

Social media posts are a rich source of content that can add authenticity and credibility to your presentation. Here are a few reasons why you might want to embed social media posts into your Sway:

1. Real-Time Updates: Embedding live social media feeds ensures that your audience receives the most current information.

2. User Engagement: Social media posts often reflect user engagement and can showcase interactions from a wide audience.

3. Visual Appeal: Social media posts often come with images, videos, and other multimedia elements that can make your presentation more visually appealing.

4. Content Variety: Embedding posts from various social media platforms can provide a diverse range of content, keeping your audience interested.

Steps to Embed Social Media Posts

Let's explore how to embed posts from some of the most popular social media platforms.

4.3.2.1 Embedding Twitter Posts

Twitter posts, or tweets, are great for embedding due to their brevity and the potential to share real-time updates. Here's how to embed a tweet:

1. Find the Tweet: Navigate to the tweet you want to embed.

2. Get the Embed Code:

   - Click on the down arrow at the top right corner of the tweet.

   - Select "Embed Tweet."

   - Copy the code provided.

3. Insert into Sway:

   - In Sway, click on the "Media" card in the Storyline.

   - Select "Embed."

   - Paste the copied embed code into the box.

   - Click "Confirm" to embed the tweet into your Sway.

4.3.2.2 Embedding Facebook Posts

Facebook posts can include text, images, and videos, making them versatile for embedding. Here's how to embed a Facebook post:

1. Find the Post: Navigate to the Facebook post you wish to embed.

2. Get the Embed Code:

   - Click on the three dots at the top right of the post.

   - Select "Embed."

   - Copy the provided code.

3. Insert into Sway:

   - In Sway, click on the "Media" card in the Storyline.

   - Select "Embed."

- Paste the copied embed code into the box.

- Click "Confirm" to embed the Facebook post into your Sway.

4.3.2.3 Embedding Instagram Posts

Instagram is a highly visual platform, and embedding Instagram posts can add a rich visual appeal to your Sway. Here's how to embed an Instagram post:

1. Find the Post: Navigate to the Instagram post you wish to embed.

2. Get the Embed Code:

   - Click on the three dots at the top right of the post.

   - Select "Embed."

   - Copy the provided code.

3. Insert into Sway:

   - In Sway, click on the "Media" card in the Storyline.

   - Select "Embed."

   - Paste the copied embed code into the box.

   - Click "Confirm" to embed the Instagram post into your Sway.

4.3.2.4 Embedding LinkedIn Posts

LinkedIn posts are great for professional content and can add value to business-related presentations. Here's how to embed a LinkedIn post:

1. Find the Post: Navigate to the LinkedIn post you want to embed.

2. Get the Embed Code:

   - Click on the three dots at the top right of the post.

   - Select "Embed this post."

   - Copy the provided code.

3. Insert into Sway:

  - In Sway, click on the "Media" card in the Storyline.

  - Select "Embed."

  - Paste the copied embed code into the box.

  - Click "Confirm" to embed the LinkedIn post into your Sway.

Tips for Embedding Social Media Posts

Embedding social media posts is straightforward, but here are some tips to ensure you get the most out of this feature:

1. Ensure Public Access: Make sure the social media posts you are embedding are public. Private or restricted posts will not be visible to your audience.

2. Use Relevant Content: Only embed posts that are relevant to the topic of your Sway. Irrelevant content can distract and confuse your audience.

3. Credit Original Authors: Always give credit to the original authors of the social media posts to maintain ethical standards and avoid plagiarism.

4. Update Regularly: Social media is dynamic, and posts can be deleted or accounts deactivated. Regularly check your embedded posts to ensure they are still live and relevant.

5. Engage with Interactive Elements: Encourage your audience to engage with the embedded social media posts by liking, sharing, or commenting directly from your Sway presentation.

Case Studies: Effective Use of Embedded Social Media Posts

To illustrate the effective use of embedded social media posts, let's look at a few case studies:

Case Study 1: Educational Presentation

A history teacher created a Sway presentation on World War II. By embedding tweets from historians and museums, the teacher provided students with real-time insights and updates on historical events and exhibits. This made the lesson more engaging and interactive, allowing students to follow historians and museums for more information.

Case Study 2: Marketing Campaign

A marketing team used Sway to present a new product launch. By embedding Instagram posts from influencers who were reviewing the product, the team was able to showcase authentic user-generated content. This added credibility to the presentation and allowed potential customers to see real-world applications of the product.

Case Study 3: Corporate Report

A company created an annual report using Sway and embedded LinkedIn posts from their executives discussing the company's achievements and future plans. This provided a professional touch to the report and allowed stakeholders to directly connect with the company's leadership on LinkedIn.

Challenges and Solutions

While embedding social media posts can enhance your Sway presentation, it's important to be aware of potential challenges and how to overcome them:

1. Broken Links: Sometimes, embedded social media posts may not display properly if the original post is deleted or the account is deactivated. Regularly check and update your embedded posts to avoid this issue.

2. Privacy Concerns: Ensure that the content you are embedding does not violate privacy policies. Use only public posts and respect the privacy of individuals.

3. Load Time: Embedding multiple social media posts can affect the load time of your Sway. Optimize your content by embedding only the most relevant posts and avoiding excessive use of multimedia.

Conclusion

Embedding social media posts in Microsoft Sway can significantly enhance the quality and engagement level of your presentations. By following the steps and best practices outlined in this section, you can effectively incorporate dynamic and interactive content into your Sway. Remember to keep your embedded content relevant, ethical, and up-to-date to ensure a seamless and engaging experience for your audience.

CHAPTER V
Design and Layout Customization

5.1 Choosing a Design

Design is a crucial aspect of any presentation, and Microsoft Sway offers a variety of tools and options to ensure your content is not only engaging but also visually appealing. In this section, we will explore how to choose and customize design themes in Sway, providing you with the knowledge to make your presentations stand out.

5.1.1 Design Themes

Design themes in Microsoft Sway serve as the foundation for the look and feel of your presentation. These themes provide predefined color schemes, fonts, and background patterns that can transform the way your content is perceived by your audience. Here's how you can choose and make the most out of Sway's design themes.

Understanding Design Themes

Design themes in Sway are more than just background colors and fonts. They encompass a holistic approach to presentation design, ensuring that every element from headings to images and text blocks are cohesively styled. When you select a theme, Sway automatically adjusts all elements within your presentation to match the chosen aesthetic.

Accessing Design Themes

To start customizing your Sway with a design theme, follow these steps:

1. Open your Sway presentation.

2. Navigate to the top right corner and click on the "Design" tab.

3. In the Design pane, you will see a selection of themes displayed. Each theme comes with a preview image, showing you a snapshot of what your Sway will look like with that theme applied.

Choosing the Right Theme

Selecting the right theme depends on the context and purpose of your presentation. Here are some considerations to keep in mind:

1. Audience: Who will be viewing your presentation? For business presentations, you might want to opt for more professional and subtle themes. For educational or creative projects, vibrant and dynamic themes could be more appropriate.

2. Content: The type of content you're presenting can also guide your theme choice. For text-heavy presentations, choose themes that offer clear and readable fonts. If your Sway includes many images, opt for themes that highlight visual elements.

3. Branding: If you're creating a presentation for a company or brand, try to choose a theme that aligns with the brand's colors and style guidelines.

Exploring Theme Options

Microsoft Sway offers a variety of themes that you can explore:

1. Default Themes: These are the standard themes provided by Sway, offering a balanced mix of professional and creative options.

2. Customizable Themes: Sway also allows you to tweak existing themes to better match your specific needs. This includes changing colors, fonts, and backgrounds.

Applying a Theme

Once you've decided on a theme, applying it is straightforward:

1. Click on the theme you want to use. Sway will automatically apply it to your entire presentation.

2. Use the "Preview" feature to see how your Sway looks with the new theme. This helps you make any necessary adjustments before finalizing your design.

Custom Design Options

If none of the default themes quite fit your needs, Sway offers a range of custom design options that allow you to tailor the look and feel of your presentation. Here's how you can customize your design:

1. Custom Colors: Sway lets you customize the color scheme of your theme. You can select a primary and secondary color that aligns with your branding or personal preference. This is particularly useful for creating a cohesive visual identity.

2. Font Choices: Sway offers various font options, allowing you to choose the typeface that best suits your content. Whether you need a formal serif font for a business report or a playful sans-serif for a creative project, Sway has options to match your needs.

3. Backgrounds and Textures: In addition to solid color backgrounds, Sway provides various textures and patterns that can add depth and interest to your presentation. You can select these from the design pane and see how they complement your overall theme.

Tips for Choosing and Customizing Themes

1. Keep It Simple: While it might be tempting to choose the most vibrant and complex theme, sometimes simplicity is key. A clean, minimalistic design can often be more effective in conveying your message without overwhelming your audience.

2. Maintain Consistency: Consistency is crucial in design. Make sure that all elements of your Sway, including colors, fonts, and images, are consistent with your chosen theme. This helps in creating a cohesive and professional look.

3. Test Different Themes: Don't be afraid to experiment with different themes. Sway allows you to preview and switch themes easily, so take advantage of this feature to find the perfect match for your presentation.

Case Study: Effective Use of Themes in Sway

Consider a scenario where you are creating a business proposal using Sway. You want your presentation to look professional yet engaging. Here's how you can effectively use themes:

1. Select a Professional Theme: Start by choosing a theme that uses neutral colors and clean fonts. This sets a formal tone for your presentation.

2. Customize Colors: Adjust the color scheme to include your company's brand colors. This reinforces your brand identity and adds a touch of personalization.

3. Use Textures Sparingly: Incorporate subtle textures in the background to add depth without distracting from the main content.

4. Consistent Fonts: Ensure that the font used for headings, subheadings, and body text is consistent throughout the presentation.

By following these steps, you create a professional and polished presentation that effectively communicates your message.

Conclusion

Choosing and customizing design themes in Microsoft Sway is a powerful way to enhance the visual appeal of your presentations. By understanding the available options and how to tailor them to your needs, you can create Sways that not only look great but also effectively convey your message. In the next section, we will explore how to adjust the layout of your Sway to further enhance its structure and readability.

5.1.2 Custom Design Options

Microsoft Sway offers a range of design customization options that allow users to create unique, visually appealing presentations. While design themes provide a solid foundation, custom design options enable you to tailor your Sway to fit specific needs and preferences. This section will explore various custom design options, including the use of colors, fonts, backgrounds, and advanced layout configurations.

1. Custom Colors and Backgrounds

Sway provides several ways to customize the colors and backgrounds of your presentation. These options allow you to align your Sway with your brand identity or personal style.

- Color Palette: You can choose a custom color palette that reflects your brand or the theme of your presentation. To access this feature, click on the "Design" tab, then select "Colors." Here, you can either select a pre-defined color scheme or create your own by choosing specific colors for the background, text, and accents.

- Background Images: Adding a custom background image can significantly enhance the visual appeal of your Sway. To add a background image, click on "Background" in the "Design" tab. You can upload an image from your device, choose from Sway's library, or search for images online. Ensure that the background image complements the overall theme and does not distract from the content.

- Texture and Patterns: For a more subtle effect, you can use textures and patterns as backgrounds. Sway offers a variety of patterns that can add depth and interest to your presentation without overwhelming the viewer.

2. Custom Fonts and Typography

Typography plays a crucial role in how your content is perceived. Sway allows you to customize the fonts to ensure your text is readable and aligns with your presentation's style.

- Font Selection: Sway provides a selection of fonts that you can use to customize the appearance of your text. To change the font, go to the "Design" tab and select "Text." Choose a font that is easy to read and appropriate for your content. For a professional look, consider using serif fonts for body text and sans-serif fonts for headings.

- Font Size and Weight: Adjusting the size and weight of the fonts can help highlight important information and create a visual hierarchy. Use larger, bolder fonts for headings and smaller, regular-weight fonts for body text. This distinction helps guide the reader's eye through the content.

- Color and Emphasis: You can further customize your text by changing its color and adding emphasis. Use a color that contrasts with the background to ensure readability. Additionally, you can use bold, italic, and underline to emphasize key points.

3. Layout and Structure

Customizing the layout and structure of your Sway allows you to organize your content in a way that is both logical and visually appealing.

- Card Layouts: Sway uses a card-based system to organize content. You can customize the layout of each card by selecting different styles, such as text, image, or group cards. To customize a card, click on it and choose from the available layout options. Experiment with different layouts to see which one best presents your information.

- Grouping and Aligning: Proper alignment and grouping of cards can make your Sway look polished and professional. Sway automatically aligns cards, but you can manually adjust them for better spacing and organization. Grouping related cards together helps create a cohesive narrative and makes it easier for the viewer to follow.

- Sections and Navigation: Dividing your Sway into sections can improve the flow and organization of your content. Sections act as chapters, allowing you to group related content together. To add a section, click on the "+" icon and select "Section." You can also customize the navigation by choosing between vertical, horizontal, or grid layouts, depending on the amount and type of content.

4. Media Customization

Incorporating media, such as images, videos, and audio, can make your Sway more engaging. Customizing how media is displayed can enhance its impact.

- Image and Video Settings: Sway allows you to adjust the settings for images and videos, including size, alignment, and captions. Click on the media to access these options. You can choose to display media in full screen, as a background, or within a card. Adding captions helps provide context and can be customized in terms of font, size, and color.

- Interactive Elements: Sway supports the inclusion of interactive elements, such as embedded content, links, and forms. These elements can be customized to fit the design of your Sway. For example, you can embed a map or social media post and adjust its size and placement. Interactive elements encourage viewer interaction and can make your presentation more dynamic.

- Audio and Narration: Adding audio or narration can provide a personal touch to your Sway. You can record audio directly within Sway or upload pre-recorded files. Customize the placement and playback settings to ensure they complement the content without being intrusive.

5. Advanced Customization with CSS

For users with some knowledge of CSS (Cascading Style Sheets), Sway offers advanced customization options that allow for more precise control over the presentation's appearance.

- Custom CSS Integration: By adding custom CSS, you can override Sway's default styles and apply your own. This feature is particularly useful for aligning your Sway with specific brand guidelines or achieving a unique look that is not possible with the built-in options. To add custom CSS, you need to access the Sway settings and input your CSS code.

- Styling Specific Elements: With CSS, you can target specific elements, such as headers, paragraphs, and media, and apply custom styles. For example, you can change the color of all headings, adjust the spacing between paragraphs, or add a border to images.

- Responsive Design: Custom CSS allows you to ensure that your Sway is responsive and looks good on all devices. By using media queries, you can adjust the layout and styles based on the screen size, providing an optimal viewing experience for both desktop and mobile users.

6. Ensuring Accessibility

Customizing your Sway also involves making it accessible to all users, including those with disabilities. Sway provides several tools and options to enhance accessibility.

- Alt Text for Images: Adding alternative text (alt text) to images ensures that screen readers can describe the content to visually impaired users. To add alt text, click on the image and enter a description in the alt text field. Ensure that the description is concise and accurately reflects the image's content.

- High Contrast Mode: Sway offers a high contrast mode that improves readability for users with visual impairments. You can enable this mode in the "Design" tab under "Accessibility."

- Keyboard Navigation: Ensuring that your Sway is navigable using a keyboard is essential for users with mobility impairments. Test your Sway to ensure that all interactive elements can be accessed and used with keyboard shortcuts.

7. Testing and Iteration

Once you have customized your Sway, it is essential to test it to ensure that it meets your expectations and works well on different devices and browsers.

- Preview Mode: Use Sway's preview mode to see how your presentation will look to viewers. This mode allows you to navigate through the Sway and make any necessary adjustments before sharing it.

- Device Testing: Check how your Sway appears on various devices, including desktops, tablets, and smartphones. Ensure that the layout is responsive and that all elements are displayed correctly.

- Feedback and Iteration: Gather feedback from colleagues or friends to identify any areas for improvement. Use this feedback to iterate on your design, making adjustments to enhance readability, engagement, and overall visual appeal.

Custom design options in Microsoft Sway provide a powerful way to create presentations that are not only informative but also visually engaging. By leveraging these customization features, you can ensure that your Sway stands out and effectively communicates your message to your audience.

5.2 Adjusting the Layout

Microsoft Sway offers a flexible and intuitive way to adjust the layout of your presentations, allowing you to tailor the visual flow to better suit your content and audience. By understanding how to manipulate the layout, you can create more engaging and effective presentations. In this section, we'll explore the two primary layout options available in Sway: vertical and horizontal. We'll also discuss the best use cases for each layout and provide tips on how to implement them effectively.

5.2.1 Vertical vs. Horizontal Layouts

Choosing the right layout for your Sway presentation is crucial for ensuring that your content is presented in the most effective and engaging way. Microsoft Sway provides two main layout options: vertical and horizontal. Each layout has its own strengths and ideal use cases, and understanding these can help you decide which layout will best serve your presentation's purpose.

Vertical Layout:

The vertical layout in Sway organizes your content in a top-to-bottom fashion. This layout is similar to a traditional webpage or a long-form article where the viewer scrolls down to see more content. The vertical layout is intuitive for most users because it mirrors the natural way we read and browse information online.

Horizontal Layout:

The horizontal layout, on the other hand, arranges content from left to right. This layout is more akin to a slideshow or a photo gallery where the viewer navigates through the content by swiping or clicking through pages horizontally. This layout can create a more dynamic and interactive experience, especially for visual-heavy content.

Choosing Between Vertical and Horizontal Layouts:

When deciding between vertical and horizontal layouts, consider the following factors:

1. Content Type:

 - Vertical Layout: Ideal for text-heavy presentations, detailed articles, step-by-step guides, or any content that benefits from a linear, scrollable format.

 - Horizontal Layout: Best suited for visual stories, portfolios, photo galleries, product showcases, or any content that benefits from a side-by-side comparison or a more dynamic browsing experience.

2. Audience Preference:

 - Consider the habits and preferences of your target audience. If your audience is accustomed to reading long-form content or browsing articles, a vertical layout might be more intuitive for them. If they prefer a more interactive and engaging experience, a horizontal layout could be more effective.

3. Presentation Context:

 - Vertical Layout: Suitable for digital documents, newsletters, blog posts, and other formats where scrolling is a natural part of the user experience.

 - Horizontal Layout: Works well for live presentations, digital portfolios, and interactive storytelling where visual impact and user interaction are paramount.

Implementing Vertical and Horizontal Layouts in Sway:

Now that we've discussed the strengths and use cases of vertical and horizontal layouts, let's delve into how you can implement these layouts in your Sway presentations.

Vertical Layout Implementation:

1. Default Vertical Layout:

 - When you create a new Sway presentation, the default layout is vertical. This means your content will be stacked one after another, and viewers will scroll down to access more information.

2. Adjusting the Vertical Layout:

- To enhance the vertical layout, you can use grouping features such as stacks, grids, and comparison cards to organize related content. This not only improves the visual appeal but also makes it easier for viewers to digest information.

3. Using Headings and Dividers:

- Utilize headings and dividers to break up sections and guide viewers through the content. Headings can serve as anchor points, while dividers provide visual breaks between different sections.

Horizontal Layout Implementation:

1. Switching to Horizontal Layout:

- To switch to a horizontal layout, go to the Design tab and select the horizontal option. This will rearrange your content into a side-by-side format.

2. Optimizing for Horizontal Navigation:

- Ensure that each section or card contains a cohesive chunk of information or a visual element that can stand on its own. This makes the horizontal navigation more intuitive and engaging.

3. Creating Interactive Experiences:

- Take advantage of Sway's interactive features, such as embed cards, to incorporate multimedia elements like videos, maps, and social media posts. These elements can make the horizontal layout more dynamic and engaging.

Best Practices for Vertical and Horizontal Layouts:

1. Consistency:

- Maintain a consistent design language throughout your presentation. Use the same fonts, colors, and visual styles to create a cohesive look and feel, regardless of the layout you choose.

2. Balance:

- Ensure a balance between text and visual elements. Too much text in a horizontal layout can make it feel cluttered, while too many visuals in a vertical layout can overwhelm the viewer.

3. Navigation Aids:

 - Incorporate navigation aids such as menus, buttons, and hyperlinks to help viewers easily move between sections, especially in longer presentations.

4. Responsive Design:

 - Test your Sway on different devices and screen sizes to ensure that your layout works well across all platforms. Both vertical and horizontal layouts should be responsive and adaptable to different viewing conditions.

5. Engagement:

 - Keep your audience engaged by using interactive elements, quizzes, and call-to-action buttons. These features can enhance the user experience and make your presentation more memorable.

Examples of Vertical and Horizontal Layouts:

To further illustrate the application of vertical and horizontal layouts, let's look at a few examples:

Vertical Layout Example:

- Educational Lesson:

 - An educational lesson on a historical event can use a vertical layout to present information chronologically. Each section can represent a different period, with images, videos, and text providing detailed explanations.

Horizontal Layout Example:

- Portfolio Showcase:

 - An artist's portfolio can benefit from a horizontal layout, where each page showcases a different project. High-quality images, project descriptions, and interactive elements can create a compelling visual narrative.

In conclusion, the choice between vertical and horizontal layouts in Microsoft Sway depends on the type of content, audience preferences, and presentation context. By understanding the strengths and use cases of each layout, you can make informed decisions that enhance the effectiveness of your presentations. Whether you opt for the intuitive scroll of a vertical layout or the dynamic interaction of a horizontal layout, Sway provides the tools you need to create engaging and impactful presentations.

5.2.2 Grouping and Aligning Cards

One of the most powerful features of Microsoft Sway is its ability to group and align cards, allowing users to create visually appealing and well-organized presentations. This section will explore the various methods for grouping and aligning cards, as well as best practices for ensuring your Sway content is both aesthetically pleasing and easy to navigate.

Understanding Card Grouping

Grouping cards in Sway is an effective way to organize related content together, making it easier for viewers to follow the flow of information. By grouping cards, you can create sections within your Sway that highlight specific themes or topics. This not only improves the visual appeal of your presentation but also enhances the overall user experience.

To group cards in Sway:

1. Select the Cards to be Grouped: Click on the first card you wish to group. Hold down the Shift key and click on additional cards to select multiple cards at once.

2. Group the Cards: Once the cards are selected, right-click and choose "Group" from the context menu. Alternatively, you can use the "Group" button in the toolbar that appears above the cards.

When cards are grouped, they are treated as a single unit. This means that any changes you make to the layout, style, or settings of the group will be applied to all cards within the group. Grouping cards is particularly useful when you want to create a consistent look and feel for a series of related pieces of content.

Types of Card Groups

Sway offers several types of card groups, each with its own unique characteristics and benefits:

1. Stack Group: This type of group arranges cards in a stack, where users can click through each card in the group one by one. Stack groups are ideal for presenting step-by-step instructions or sequential content.

2. Grid Group: Grid groups display cards in a grid layout, allowing viewers to see multiple cards at once. This layout is useful for showcasing collections of images, products, or articles.

3. Comparison Group: Comparison groups are designed to compare two pieces of content side by side. This is perfect for highlighting differences or similarities between two items.

4. Slideshow Group: Slideshow groups present cards as a slideshow, where users can navigate through the cards using arrows. This is a great option for creating visual presentations or portfolios.

To create a specific type of group, follow these steps:

1. Select the Cards: As previously mentioned, select the cards you wish to group.

2. Choose the Group Type: Right-click the selected cards, choose "Group," and then select the desired group type from the submenu.

Aligning Cards

Alignment is crucial for creating a polished and professional-looking Sway presentation. Properly aligned cards help guide the viewer's eye and make the content more readable and aesthetically pleasing.

Aligning Cards Horizontally:

1. Select the Cards: Click and drag to select the cards you want to align.

2. Use the Alignment Tool: In the toolbar that appears above the selected cards, click the "Align" button and choose the desired alignment option (e.g., left, center, right).

Aligning Cards Vertically:

1. Select the Cards: Click and drag to select the cards you want to align.

2. Use the Alignment Tool: In the toolbar, click the "Align" button and choose the vertical alignment option (e.g., top, middle, bottom).

Sway's alignment tools ensure that your cards are evenly spaced and aligned, creating a clean and organized look for your presentation.

Best Practices for Grouping and Aligning Cards

To make the most of Sway's grouping and alignment features, consider the following best practices:

1. Consistent Grouping: Use consistent grouping throughout your Sway to maintain a uniform structure. For example, if you use stack groups for instructional content, continue using stack groups for similar sections.

2. Balanced Layouts: Aim for balanced layouts that distribute content evenly across the screen. Avoid overcrowding one side of the presentation, as this can make it look cluttered.

3. Visual Hierarchy: Establish a visual hierarchy by grouping related content and aligning cards in a way that guides the viewer's eye. Use larger cards for important information and smaller cards for supporting details.

4. Whitespace: Don't be afraid to use whitespace to separate different sections and prevent the presentation from appearing too busy. Proper use of whitespace can enhance readability and visual appeal.

5. Alignment Guides: Utilize Sway's alignment guides to ensure precise positioning of cards. These guides help you line up cards accurately, making the layout look professional.

Examples of Effective Grouping and Alignment

Example 1: Product Showcase

Imagine you are creating a Sway presentation to showcase a series of products. You could use grid groups to display images of each product, with accompanying text cards providing details about each item. By aligning the text cards consistently below each image, you create a cohesive and easy-to-navigate product showcase.

Example 2: Educational Lesson

For an educational lesson, you might use stack groups to present a step-by-step guide on a particular topic. Each card in the stack group could represent a different step, with images and text explaining the process. By aligning the cards centrally and ensuring equal spacing, you create a clear and organized lesson plan.

Example 3: Travel Journal

If you're creating a travel journal in Sway, you could use a combination of stack and slideshow groups. Stack groups could be used to present daily entries, while slideshow groups could showcase photo galleries from different locations. By aligning the entries and photo galleries consistently, you create a visually appealing and immersive travel journal.

Advanced Techniques for Grouping and Aligning

While Sway provides a range of tools for grouping and aligning cards, advanced users can take their presentations to the next level with custom CSS and additional design techniques.

Custom CSS:

For those familiar with CSS, Sway allows the use of custom CSS to further refine the appearance and alignment of cards. By adding custom CSS, you can achieve precise control over spacing, fonts, colors, and other design elements. To use custom CSS:

1. Access the Design Tab: Click on the Design tab in the top navigation bar.

2. Open the Customization Panel: Click the "Customize" button to open the customization panel.

3. Add Custom CSS: In the panel, enter your custom CSS code to adjust the layout and style of your cards.

Advanced Design Techniques:

1. Overlaying Text on Images: Create dynamic and engaging presentations by overlaying text on images. This technique draws attention to key points and enhances the visual appeal of your Sway.

2. Interactive Elements: Incorporate interactive elements such as buttons and hyperlinks to guide viewers through your presentation and encourage engagement.

3. Consistent Color Scheme: Use a consistent color scheme throughout your Sway to create a cohesive and professional look. Choose colors that complement each other and enhance readability.

Conclusion

Mastering the art of grouping and aligning cards in Microsoft Sway is essential for creating visually appealing and well-organized presentations. By understanding the different types of card groups and utilizing alignment tools effectively, you can enhance the overall aesthetic and usability of your Sway content. Remember to follow best practices for consistent grouping, balanced layouts, and visual hierarchy to ensure your presentations are both professional and engaging. With these skills, you'll be well on your way to creating stunning Sway presentations that captivate and inform your audience.

5.3 Advanced Design Techniques

5.3.1 Using the Remix Feature

The Remix feature in Microsoft Sway is a powerful tool that allows users to automatically generate a fresh and engaging design for their presentations. This feature is particularly useful for those who may not have a background in design or who are looking to quickly create a visually appealing presentation without spending too much time on manual customization. In this section, we'll delve into the details of how to use the Remix feature effectively, explore its benefits, and provide some tips on how to make the most of this innovative tool.

What is the Remix Feature?

The Remix feature is an automated design tool within Microsoft Sway that helps users quickly apply different design themes and layouts to their content. By clicking the Remix button, Sway will automatically rearrange and style the content in your Sway, offering a new and unique look each time. This feature leverages the power of algorithms to create visually pleasing presentations, taking into account the type and amount of content you have added.

How to Use the Remix Feature

Using the Remix feature is straightforward and can be done with just a few clicks. Here is a step-by-step guide on how to use it:

1. Open Your Sway: Start by opening the Sway you want to remix. Ensure that you have added all the necessary content, including text, images, videos, and other media.

2. Locate the Remix Button: The Remix button is located in the top right corner of the Sway interface. It is easily recognizable and labeled clearly.

3. Click the Remix Button: Simply click the Remix button. Sway will then process the content and apply a new design theme and layout.

4. Review the Changes: After the Remix process is complete, review the new design. Take note of any elements that you particularly like or dislike.

5. Repeat if Necessary: If you are not satisfied with the new design, you can click the Remix button again to generate another version. You can repeat this process as many times as needed until you find a design that suits your preferences.

Benefits of Using the Remix Feature

The Remix feature offers several benefits, especially for users who are looking to create professional-looking presentations quickly and efficiently. Here are some of the key advantages:

1. Time-Saving: Remixing can save a significant amount of time by automating the design process. Instead of manually adjusting each element, users can rely on Sway's algorithms to create a cohesive and attractive presentation.

2. Design Inspiration: For users who are unsure about how to design their presentation, the Remix feature can provide inspiration. By generating different layouts and themes, it can help users visualize various design possibilities.

3. Consistency: The Remix feature ensures that the design remains consistent throughout the presentation. This is particularly important for maintaining a professional look and feel.

4. User-Friendly: The feature is easy to use, even for those with little to no design experience. The straightforward interface and one-click functionality make it accessible to all users.

Tips for Effective Use of the Remix Feature

While the Remix feature is powerful, there are a few tips that can help users get the most out of it:

1. Start with Quality Content: The effectiveness of the Remix feature depends largely on the quality of the content you provide. Ensure that your text, images, and other media are well-organized and relevant.

2. Be Open to Experimentation: Don't be afraid to click the Remix button multiple times. Each click can generate a completely new design, so explore different options until you find the perfect one.

3. Customize After Remixing: While the Remix feature does a great job of creating a base design, consider making additional customizations to fine-tune the presentation. This can include adjusting colors, fonts, and layout details.

4. Pay Attention to Readability: Ensure that the remixed design maintains readability and clarity. Sometimes, automatic designs may look visually appealing but can compromise on the readability of the content.

5. Consider Your Audience: Keep your audience in mind when using the Remix feature. Different designs may appeal to different audiences, so choose a style that aligns with the preferences and expectations of your viewers.

Example Use Case: Business Presentation

Let's consider an example to illustrate the use of the Remix feature. Imagine you are creating a business presentation on the annual performance of your company. You have gathered all the necessary data, including charts, graphs, and key metrics. Here's how you could use the Remix feature:

1. Add Content: First, you add all your text, images, and charts into Sway. Ensure that each piece of content is on its respective card.

2. Initial Design: You start with a basic design to ensure all content is added correctly.

3. Click Remix: Once the content is complete, you click the Remix button. Sway generates a new design, organizing the content into a professional layout with appropriate styles and themes.

4. Review and Adjust: You review the new design and notice that while the overall look is great, some charts need repositioning for better emphasis. You make these minor adjustments manually.

5. Finalize: After a few iterations, you find a design that perfectly matches your needs. You finalize the presentation and prepare to share it with your stakeholders.

Example Use Case: Educational Project

Now, let's consider a different scenario where you are a teacher creating an interactive lesson for your students on the topic of climate change:

1. Content Preparation: You gather various types of content, including informational text, images of climate events, videos of scientific explanations, and interactive maps.

2. Initial Setup: You organize all the content into Sway, ensuring each type of media is correctly placed on different cards.

3. Engage the Remix Feature: To make the lesson visually appealing, you use the Remix feature. After clicking the Remix button, Sway generates a dynamic layout that includes all your content in an engaging manner.

4. Iterate and Customize: You go through several iterations of remixing until you find a design that is both educational and visually stimulating for your students. You make a few manual adjustments to highlight key points.

5. Present: The final product is an interactive and visually appealing lesson on climate change, ready to be presented to your class.

Conclusion

The Remix feature in Microsoft Sway is an invaluable tool for users looking to create professional and engaging presentations with minimal effort. By leveraging the power of automated design, it allows users to explore various styles and layouts quickly and easily. Whether you are creating business presentations, educational projects, or personal stories, the Remix feature can help you achieve a polished and visually appealing result. Remember to start with quality content, be open to experimentation, and make additional customizations to ensure your presentation meets your specific needs and preferences. With these tips and techniques, you can harness the full potential of the Remix feature and create stunning presentations that captivate your audience.

5.3.2 Customizing with CSS

Customizing your Sway presentation with CSS (Cascading Style Sheets) can take your design to the next level by allowing you to apply more precise and creative styles to your content. Although Sway doesn't directly support CSS within its interface, you can still embed HTML and CSS code snippets to achieve the desired effects. This section will guide you through the basics of using CSS to enhance your Sway presentations.

Understanding CSS

CSS is a style sheet language used to describe the presentation of a document written in HTML. It allows you to specify how elements should be rendered on screen, in print, or in other media. CSS provides a powerful tool for controlling the layout, colors, fonts, and other visual aspects of your content.

Key Concepts of CSS:

- Selectors: Target specific HTML elements to apply styles to them.

- Properties: Define what aspect of the element you want to change, such as color, font-size, margin, etc.

- Values: Specify the exact value for the property, such as `red` for color, `16px` for font-size, etc.

Integrating CSS in Sway

Since Sway primarily focuses on ease of use and does not provide a native CSS editor, you can use HTML cards to embed custom CSS. Here's how to do it:

1. Create an HTML Card: Add a new card and select the "Embed" option. Here, you can insert your HTML code that includes embedded CSS.

2. Write Your CSS Code: Within the HTML card, use the `<style>` tag to include your CSS styles. For example:

```html
<style>
  h1 {
    color: blue;
    font-size: 36px;
  }
```

```
p {

  font-family: Arial, sans-serif;

  line-height: 1.5;

}

.custom-button {

  background-color: green;

  color: white;

  padding: 10px 20px;

  border: none;

  border-radius: 5px;

}

</style>
```

3. Apply CSS to HTML Elements: Include the HTML elements within the same card or other cards in Sway that you want to style. For example:

```html
<h1>My Custom Header</h1>

<p>This is a paragraph with custom styling.</p>

<button class="custom-button">Click Me</button>
```

Examples of CSS Customizations

Here are some practical examples of how you can use CSS to enhance your Sway presentations:

1. Custom Fonts and Colors:

```html
<style>
  body {
    font-family: 'Roboto', sans-serif;
    background-color: f0f0f0;
  }
  h1 {
    color: 333333;
    font-size: 48px;
  }
</style>
<h1>Welcome to My Sway Presentation</h1>
```

2. Responsive Layouts:

```html
<style>
  .container {
    display: flex;
    flex-wrap: wrap;
  }
  .box {
```

```html
    flex: 1 1 200px;

    margin: 10px;

    padding: 20px;

    background-color: e0e0e0;

  }

</style>

<div class="container">

  <div class="box">Box 1</div>

  <div class="box">Box 2</div>

  <div class="box">Box 3</div>

</div>

```
```

3. Animations:

```html

<style>

  .fade-in {

    animation: fadeIn 2s ease-in-out;

  }

  @keyframes fadeIn {

    from { opacity: 0; }

    to { opacity: 1; }

  }

</style>
```
```

```
<p class="fade-in">This text will fade in.</p>

```

Best Practices for Using CSS in Sway

While CSS offers a wide range of possibilities, it's important to follow best practices to ensure your customizations enhance rather than detract from your Sway presentations:

1. Keep it Simple: Avoid overly complex styles that can slow down the loading time or make your content difficult to read.

2. Test Across Devices: Make sure your custom styles look good on various devices and screen sizes.

3. Consistency: Maintain a consistent design language throughout your presentation to provide a cohesive experience.

4. Accessibility: Ensure that your styles do not hinder the accessibility of your content. For example, avoid low contrast color schemes that can be difficult to read for some users.

Troubleshooting CSS Issues

When integrating custom CSS into your Sway presentations, you might encounter some issues. Here are some common problems and their solutions:

1. CSS Not Applying:

  - Ensure that your CSS selectors correctly target the elements you want to style.

  - Check for any syntax errors in your CSS code.

2. Styles Not Rendering Correctly:

  - Verify that your CSS is compatible with the HTML structure in Sway.

  - Use browser developer tools to inspect and debug your styles.

3. Conflicting Styles:

  - Be aware that Sway's default styles might override your custom CSS. Use more specific selectors or the `!important` declaration to ensure your styles are applied.

Advanced CSS Techniques

For those looking to push the boundaries further, here are some advanced CSS techniques that can add a unique touch to your Sway presentations:

1. Custom CSS Frameworks:

  - Utilize CSS frameworks like Bootstrap or Foundation to quickly implement complex layouts and components.

2. CSS Grid and Flexbox:

  - Leverage CSS Grid and Flexbox for more flexible and responsive design layouts.

3. Pseudo-Elements and Classes:

  - Use pseudo-elements (`::before`, `::after`) and pseudo-classes (`:hover`, `:focus`) to add decorative and interactive elements.

4. Variables and Custom Properties:

  - Utilize CSS variables for more maintainable and reusable styles.

```html
<style>
  :root {
    --main-bg-color: ff6347;
    --main-text-color: ffffff;
  }
  body {
    background-color: var(--main-bg-color);
    color: var(--main-text-color);
  }
</style>
```

Conclusion

Customizing your Sway presentations with CSS allows you to transcend the basic design options provided by the platform, enabling you to create visually stunning and highly personalized content. By embedding CSS through HTML cards, you can manipulate the appearance and layout of your Sway to better align with your creative vision or branding requirements.

Remember, while CSS is a powerful tool, it is important to use it judiciously to enhance the user experience rather than complicate it. Follow best practices, keep accessibility in mind, and continually test your designs across different devices to ensure they deliver the impact you desire.

With the knowledge and techniques covered in this section, you are now equipped to take full control of your Sway presentations, making them more engaging and visually appealing to your audience. Happy customizing!

CHAPTER VI
Sharing and Collaborating

6.1 Sharing Your Sway

Creating a compelling and visually engaging Sway is only the beginning. To fully leverage the power of Microsoft Sway, you need to share your creations effectively. Sharing your Sway allows you to present your ideas, stories, or reports to your intended audience, whether they are colleagues, students, or friends. Understanding the various sharing options and settings is crucial to ensure your content is accessible and secure.

6.1.1 Sharing Settings

Sharing settings in Microsoft Sway provide you with the control over who can view and interact with your content. These settings are essential for maintaining privacy, security, and collaboration standards. Let's delve into the different sharing settings available in Sway and how to configure them to suit your needs.

1. Accessing Sharing Settings

To access the sharing settings, you first need to navigate to your Sway. Open the Sway you want to share and click on the "Share" button located in the upper-right corner of the screen. This will open a panel with various sharing options.

2. Sharing with Specific People

One of the most secure ways to share your Sway is by limiting access to specific people. This option ensures that only individuals you invite can view or edit your Sway. Here's how to set it up:

- Invite by Email: In the sharing panel, select the option to "Invite people." Enter the email addresses of the individuals you want to invite. You can separate multiple email addresses with commas. After entering the email addresses, click "Invite." The recipients will receive an email invitation with a link to access your Sway.

- Permissions: You can set different levels of access for each invitee. There are two primary permissions you can grant:

  - View Only: Recipients can only view the Sway but cannot make any changes.

  - Edit: Recipients can view and make changes to the Sway. This is useful for collaborative projects where multiple contributors need to edit the content.

3. Anyone with a Link

If you prefer a more open approach, you can set your Sway so that anyone with the link can view or edit it. This method is less secure than sharing with specific people but can be convenient for broader distribution. Here's how to configure it:

- Generate Link: In the sharing panel, select the option for "Anyone with a link." You will be presented with two sub-options:

  - View Only Link: Click on "View link" to generate a link that allows anyone with the link to view your Sway. Copy the link and share it via email, social media, or any other platform.

  - Edit Link: Click on "Edit link" to generate a link that allows anyone with the link to edit your Sway. This is useful for collaborative projects where you want feedback or contributions from multiple people. Copy the link and share it accordingly.

- Revoking Access: If at any point you want to revoke access to your Sway, you can disable the link. Go back to the sharing panel and turn off the link sharing option. This will invalidate the previously generated link, and no one will be able to access your Sway through it.

4. Organizational Sharing

For business and educational institutions using Microsoft 365, Sway offers organizational sharing settings. This allows you to restrict access to people within your organization, providing a balance between accessibility and security. Here's how to set it up:

- Organization Access: In the sharing panel, select the option for "People in your organization." This setting ensures that only individuals with a valid organizational account (e.g., your company or school email) can access the Sway.

- Permissions: Similar to sharing with specific people, you can set permissions for organizational sharing:

  - View Only: Individuals within your organization can view the Sway but cannot make changes.

  - Edit: Individuals within your organization can view and edit the Sway. This is ideal for internal projects that require collaboration.

5. Social Media and Embed Code

Sway also provides options to share your content on social media platforms or embed it on websites. These methods increase the reach of your Sway and allow you to integrate it into other online spaces. Here's how to use these features:

- Social Media Sharing: In the sharing panel, you will see icons for various social media platforms such as Facebook, Twitter, and LinkedIn. Click on the relevant icon to share your Sway directly on that platform. You may need to log in to your social media account and customize your post before sharing.

- Embed Code: To embed your Sway on a website or blog, select the option for "Get embed code" in the sharing panel. This will generate an HTML code snippet that you can copy and paste into your website's code. The embed code allows visitors to view your Sway directly on your site without having to navigate away.

6. Password Protection

For an additional layer of security, Microsoft Sway allows you to set a password for your Sway. This ensures that only individuals with the password can access the content. Here's how to set it up:

- Enable Password Protection: In the sharing panel, look for the option to "Set a password." Enter a strong password and save the settings. Share this password only with individuals you want to grant access to.

- Accessing Password-Protected Sway: When someone tries to access your password-protected Sway, they will be prompted to enter the password. Without the correct password, they will not be able to view the content.

7. Managing Shared Sways

It's important to periodically review and manage the sharing settings of your Sways to ensure they remain secure and accessible only to the intended audience. Here are some best practices:

- Review Permissions: Regularly check who has access to your Sways and update permissions as needed. Remove access for individuals who no longer need it.

- Update Links: If you suspect that a link has been shared with unauthorized individuals, generate a new link and distribute it to the intended audience.

- Monitor Collaborators: For Sways with multiple collaborators, keep track of who has edit permissions and ensure that all contributors are actively involved in the project.

Conclusion

Understanding and effectively using sharing settings in Microsoft Sway is essential for protecting your content and ensuring it reaches the right audience. Whether you're sharing with specific individuals, your organization, or the public, Sway provides a range of options to meet your needs. By configuring these settings appropriately, you can maintain control over your Sway while facilitating collaboration and engagement.

6.1.2 Generating a Shareable Link

Sharing your Sway presentation is a straightforward process that allows you to distribute your content widely and efficiently. Generating a shareable link is one of the most effective ways to share your Sway with others, whether it's for educational purposes, business presentations, or personal projects. This section will guide you through the steps to create a shareable link, adjust privacy settings, and ensure that your audience can access your content seamlessly.

Step-by-Step Guide to Generating a Shareable Link

Step 1: Open Your Sway

To begin, log in to your Microsoft account and navigate to the Sway dashboard. Locate the Sway you wish to share from the list of your Sways. Click on the Sway to open it in the editor.

Step 2: Access the Share Menu

Once your Sway is open, look for the "Share" button, usually located in the upper-right corner of the screen. Clicking on this button will open the sharing options.

Step 3: Choose the Shareable Link Option

In the Share menu, you will see several sharing options, including email, social media, and embed code. To generate a shareable link, select the "Get a link" option. This will create a unique URL that you can distribute to others.

Step 4: Adjust Link Settings

Before you finalize the link, you can adjust the settings to control who can view or edit your Sway. Microsoft Sway provides several options for link settings:

- Anyone with the link: This setting allows anyone who has the link to view your Sway. It's the most open option and is ideal for sharing your Sway widely without restrictions.

- People in your organization: This setting restricts access to people within your organization. They must be logged into their organizational account to view the Sway.

- Specific people: This option allows you to specify particular individuals who can view or edit your Sway. You will need to enter their email addresses.

Step 5: Copy the Link

Once you have chosen the appropriate settings, click on the "Create" or "Copy" button next to the generated link. This will copy the link to your clipboard, making it ready to paste wherever you need it.

Step 6: Distribute the Link

Paste the copied link into an email, a social media post, a chat message, or any other medium you prefer for sharing. Recipients can click on the link to access your Sway directly.

Customizing Your Shareable Link

To ensure your Sway reaches the intended audience and meets your sharing goals, you might consider customizing the link further. Here are some additional customization options:

1. Shortening the Link

For ease of use, especially in social media or printed materials, you might want to shorten the link. Services like Bitly, TinyURL, or even Microsoft's own shortening tools can help you create a more manageable link.

2. Adding Password Protection

For an extra layer of security, you can add password protection to your Sway link. This ensures that only people with the password can view your content. While this feature isn't directly available within Sway, you can use third-party services to password-protect the link.

3. Tracking Link Clicks

If you want to monitor how many people are viewing your Sway, you can use link-tracking services. These services provide analytics on how many times the link is clicked, where the clicks are coming from, and other valuable metrics. This is particularly useful for business presentations or marketing campaigns.

Best Practices for Sharing Your Sway

1. Clear Communication

When sharing your Sway, provide a brief description or introduction along with the link. This helps recipients understand the content and context of the Sway before they click on the link.

2. Testing the Link

Before distributing the link widely, test it yourself. Open the link in a different browser or on a different device to ensure it works correctly and displays your Sway as intended.

3. Regular Updates

If your Sway content is dynamic and changes frequently, make sure to update your audience. You can resend the link with a note about the new content or updates to keep your audience engaged.

4. Feedback and Interaction

Encourage feedback and interaction from your audience. Sway allows viewers to comment and interact with the content. Use these features to gather insights and improve your presentations.

Troubleshooting Link Issues

Sometimes, recipients might encounter issues when trying to access your Sway through the shareable link. Here are common problems and solutions:

1. Link Not Working

If recipients report that the link is not working, ensure that the link settings allow access to the intended audience. Check that the link was copied correctly and wasn't truncated or altered.

2. Permission Denied

If viewers receive a "permission denied" message, verify the privacy settings. Ensure that the link settings match your sharing intentions (e.g., "Anyone with the link" vs. "Specific people").

3. Browser Compatibility

Occasionally, certain browsers might have issues rendering Sway content. Recommend that viewers try accessing the link using a different browser or updating their current browser to the latest version.

4. Network Restrictions

In some cases, organizational or network restrictions might block access to external links. Advise viewers to try accessing the link from a different network or contact their IT department for assistance.

Enhancing Engagement with Shareable Links

To maximize the impact of your shared Sway, consider these strategies to enhance engagement:

1. Interactive Elements

Incorporate interactive elements such as polls, quizzes, or embedded forms within your Sway. This encourages viewers to engage with the content actively rather than passively consuming information.

2. Multimedia Content

Leverage the multimedia capabilities of Sway by including videos, audio clips, and high-quality images. Diverse content types can make your Sway more engaging and visually appealing.

3. Clear Call-to-Action

Include a clear call-to-action (CTA) in your Sway. Whether it's signing up for a newsletter, participating in a survey, or contacting you for more information, a strong CTA can drive viewer interaction and achieve your objectives.

4. Follow-Up Communication

After sharing your Sway, follow up with your audience. Send a thank-you note, ask for feedback, or provide additional resources. This maintains engagement and fosters a sense of community around your content.

Case Studies: Successful Use of Shareable Links

Case Study 1: Educational Use

A high school teacher used Sway to create an interactive history project. By generating a shareable link, the teacher distributed the project to students, parents, and other teachers.

The Sway included videos, timelines, and interactive maps. The teacher received positive feedback and noted an increase in student engagement.

Case Study 2: Business Presentation

A marketing team used Sway to prepare a product launch presentation. By sharing the Sway link with potential clients and stakeholders, they provided an interactive overview of the new product features, benefits, and market positioning. The shareable link allowed the marketing team to reach a broader audience and facilitated real-time feedback during the launch event.

Case Study 3: Nonprofit Campaign

A nonprofit organization used Sway to create an awareness campaign about environmental conservation. They shared the Sway link on social media and via email newsletters. The interactive elements, including embedded donation forms and volunteer sign-up sheets, resulted in increased donations and volunteer sign-ups.

Conclusion

Generating a shareable link in Microsoft Sway is a powerful tool for distributing your presentations and engaging with your audience. By following the steps outlined in this section, you can create, customize, and distribute links effectively, ensuring that your Sway reaches and resonates with your intended audience. Whether you're using Sway for education, business, or personal projects, mastering the art of sharing will enhance the impact and reach of your content.

6.2 Collaboration Features

6.2.1 Inviting Collaborators

Collaborating in Microsoft Sway can enhance productivity, creativity, and ensure that your projects benefit from multiple perspectives. Inviting collaborators allows multiple people to edit and contribute to a single Sway, making it a powerful tool for group projects, team presentations, and collaborative content creation. This section will guide you through the process of inviting collaborators to your Sway, ensuring a smooth and effective collaboration experience.

Step-by-Step Guide to Inviting Collaborators

Step 1: Open Your Sway

1. Access Your Sway: Log in to your Microsoft account and navigate to the Sway website. Once logged in, find and open the Sway you want to collaborate on.

2. Navigate to the Sway: If you have many Sways, use the search bar or browse through the "My Sways" section to locate the correct one.

Step 2: Access Collaboration Options

1. Open the Sharing Menu: Click on the "Share" button located at the top-right corner of the Sway interface. This will open a menu with several sharing and collaboration options.

2. Select Collaboration Settings: In the sharing menu, you will see an option that says "Invite people to edit". Click on this option to open the collaboration settings.

Step 3: Invite Collaborators

1. Enter Email Addresses: In the collaboration settings, you will find a field where you can enter the email addresses of the people you want to invite. Type in the email addresses, separating each with a comma or pressing the enter key after each one.

2. Set Permissions: Decide what level of access you want to give your collaborators. Typically, you will have the option to allow full editing capabilities. Make sure you understand the implications of these permissions before proceeding.

3. Add a Message (Optional): You can add a personal message to your invite, explaining the purpose of the collaboration or any specific instructions. This can be particularly helpful for providing context or highlighting areas where you need input.

Step 4: Send Invitations

1. Send the Invite: Once you have entered the email addresses and set the permissions, click on the "Invite" button. This will send an invitation to the specified email addresses, allowing the recipients to access and edit your Sway.

2. Confirm Invitations: You will receive a confirmation that your invitations have been sent. Recipients will receive an email with a link to access the Sway.

Managing Collaborator Permissions

Viewing Collaborators

1. Access the Collaborators List: At any time, you can view a list of all current collaborators by going to the "Share" menu and selecting "View Collaborators". This list will show the email addresses of everyone who has access to your Sway.

2. Check Permissions: Next to each collaborator's name, you will see their permission level. This can help you keep track of who has editing rights and make adjustments if necessary.

Changing Permissions

1. Edit Permissions: To change a collaborator's permissions, click on the drop-down menu next to their email address in the collaborators list. You can upgrade or downgrade their access as needed.

2. Remove Collaborators: If you need to revoke access, you can remove a collaborator by clicking the "Remove" or "Revoke Access" button next to their email address. This will immediately prevent them from editing the Sway.

Collaboration Best Practices

Communicating with Collaborators

1. Set Expectations: Before inviting collaborators, communicate clearly about the goals of the project, the expected contributions, and any deadlines. This can help prevent misunderstandings and ensure everyone is on the same page.

2. Regular Updates: Use the message feature in the invitation to provide initial instructions and continue to communicate regularly through email or a messaging platform to keep everyone informed of updates and changes.

Organizing Content

1. Assign Sections: If your Sway is large or complex, consider assigning specific sections or topics to different collaborators. This can streamline the editing process and ensure that all areas receive attention.

2. Use Comments: Encourage collaborators to use the comment feature within Sway to leave notes, suggestions, or feedback. This can help facilitate discussion and make it easier to incorporate changes.

Tracking Changes

1. Version Control: Keep track of major changes by periodically saving copies of your Sway or noting significant updates in a shared document. This can help you revert to earlier versions if needed.

2. Reviewing Edits: Regularly review the changes made by collaborators to ensure they align with the overall vision and quality standards of the project. Address any issues promptly to maintain a cohesive final product.

Common Challenges and Solutions

Conflict Resolution

1. Conflicting Edits: If multiple collaborators are working on the same section simultaneously, conflicting edits can occur. Encourage collaborators to communicate and coordinate their editing times or use comments to propose changes before implementing them.

2. Differing Opinions: In collaborative projects, differing opinions are natural. Foster an environment of open communication and respect, and be willing to compromise or seek consensus when necessary.

Technical Issues

1. Access Problems: If a collaborator is having trouble accessing the Sway, check their invitation status and ensure the link is correct. Sometimes resending the invitation can resolve access issues.

2. Editing Lag: If multiple people are editing simultaneously, there may be some lag. Encourage collaborators to save their work frequently and be patient with any delays.

Ensuring Security

1. Secure Links: Only share the collaboration link with trusted individuals. Avoid posting it in public forums or unsecured platforms.

2. Regular Review: Periodically review the list of collaborators and their permissions to ensure that only current and necessary individuals have access. Remove any former collaborators who no longer need access.

Utilizing Collaboration Tools

Built-in Features

1. Real-time Editing: Take advantage of Sway's real-time editing feature to see changes as they happen. This can help you stay informed of updates and provide immediate feedback.

2. Comments and Suggestions: Use the comments and suggestions features within Sway to facilitate discussion and gather input from collaborators.

External Tools

1. Communication Platforms: Use external communication platforms like Microsoft Teams, Slack, or email to coordinate with collaborators, share updates, and discuss changes.

2. Project Management Tools: For larger projects, consider using project management tools like Trello, Asana, or Microsoft Planner to assign tasks, track progress, and manage deadlines.

Finalizing the Collaboration

Review and Approval

1. Final Review: Before finalizing your Sway, conduct a thorough review of all content. Check for consistency, accuracy, and completeness.

2. Approval Process: If necessary, establish an approval process where key stakeholders can review and approve the final version before it is shared or published.

Publishing and Sharing

1. Publish the Sway: Once all collaborators have completed their contributions and the final review is done, publish the Sway by selecting the "Share" button and choosing the appropriate sharing settings.

2. Distribute the Link: Share the link with your intended audience, whether it's a public presentation, a team report, or a classroom project.

Celebrating Success

1. Acknowledge Contributions: Take the time to acknowledge and thank all collaborators for their contributions. This can be done in the Sway itself or through a separate communication.

2. Reflect on the Process: After the project is complete, reflect on the collaboration process. Discuss what worked well and what could be improved for future projects.

By following these steps and best practices, you can effectively invite collaborators to your Sway and manage the collaboration process smoothly. This will ensure that your projects benefit from the collective expertise and creativity of your team, resulting in a high-quality and engaging final product.

6.2.2 Managing Permissions

Managing permissions in Microsoft Sway is an essential part of ensuring that your content is viewed and edited by the right audience. Whether you are working on a collaborative project or sharing your Sway with a wider audience, understanding how to manage permissions effectively will help maintain control over your content.

Understanding Permission Levels

Microsoft Sway offers several permission levels that determine who can view or edit your Sway. These permissions can be categorized into three main types:

1. View Only: Recipients can only view the Sway and cannot make any changes.

2. Edit: Recipients can view and edit the Sway.

3. Owner: Full control over the Sway, including sharing settings and permissions.

Each of these permission levels serves different purposes depending on your sharing needs.

Setting Permissions for Your Sway

To set permissions for your Sway, follow these steps:

1. Open the Sway you want to manage permissions for: Navigate to the Sway dashboard and select the Sway you want to share.

2. Click on the "Share" button: This is usually located at the top right corner of the Sway interface.

3. Choose your sharing option: Decide whether you want to share with specific people or groups, or generate a link that can be shared more broadly.

4. Set the permission level: When generating a link or sharing with specific individuals, you can select the appropriate permission level (view or edit).

Sharing with Specific Individuals

When you want to share your Sway with specific people, you can add their email addresses directly in the sharing settings. This method is useful for collaborative projects where you need to control who has access to edit or view the Sway.

1. Click on "Share": Open the sharing options by clicking the "Share" button.

2. Select "Specific people": Choose the option to share with specific individuals.

3. Enter email addresses: Add the email addresses of the people you want to share the Sway with.

4. Set permissions: Choose whether these individuals can view or edit the Sway.

5. Send invitations: Click on the "Send" button to send the sharing invitations.

Generating a Shareable Link

If you prefer to share your Sway with a broader audience, you can generate a shareable link. This link can be sent via email, posted on social media, or embedded on a website. When generating a link, you can still control the permissions to ensure that only the desired level of access is granted.

1. Click on "Share": Access the sharing options.

2. Choose "Anyone with a link": Select this option to generate a shareable link.

3. Set permissions: Choose whether people with the link can view or edit the Sway.

4. Copy the link: Click on the "Copy link" button to copy the generated link to your clipboard.

5. Distribute the link: Share the link via email, social media, or embed it in a website.

Managing Existing Permissions

Managing permissions for an existing Sway is crucial for maintaining control over who can access and modify your content. You can adjust permissions at any time by following these steps:

1. Open the Sway: Navigate to the Sway you want to manage.

2. Click on "Share": Open the sharing settings.

3. Review current permissions: Look at the list of people and links that have access to your Sway.

4. Adjust individual permissions: For specific individuals, you can change their permission level or remove their access altogether.

5. Update link permissions: If you have generated a shareable link, you can modify the permissions for the link or disable it entirely.

Revoking Access

If you need to revoke access for certain individuals or links, you can do so easily. This is useful if someone no longer needs access or if you need to tighten security on your Sway.

1. Open the Sway: Go to the Sway from which you want to revoke access.

2. Click on "Share": Access the sharing settings.

3. Identify the individual or link: Find the person or link you want to revoke access from.

4. Revoke access: Click on the "Remove" or "Revoke access" button next to the individual or link.

Best Practices for Managing Permissions

Effectively managing permissions in Microsoft Sway ensures that your content is secure and only accessible by the intended audience. Here are some best practices:

1. Regularly review permissions: Periodically check who has access to your Sway and adjust permissions as necessary.

2. Use specific sharing options for sensitive content: For sensitive or confidential content, share with specific individuals rather than generating a broad link.

3. Educate collaborators on proper use: Ensure that collaborators understand the importance of permissions and how to manage them.

4. Disable links when no longer needed: If a shareable link is no longer needed, disable it to prevent unauthorized access.

5. Keep track of changes: Use Sway's version history and analytics to monitor changes and access patterns.

Collaboration Etiquette

When collaborating with others on a Sway, it's important to follow good etiquette to ensure smooth and effective teamwork:

1. Communicate clearly: Use comments or notes within Sway to communicate with collaborators about changes or suggestions.

2. Respect others' contributions: Value and acknowledge the contributions of other team members.

3. Set clear roles and permissions: Define roles and permissions from the outset to avoid confusion and overlap.

4. Regularly update collaborators: Keep everyone informed about significant changes or updates to the Sway.

Troubleshooting Permission Issues

Occasionally, you might encounter issues with permissions in Microsoft Sway. Here are some common problems and how to resolve them:

1. Collaborator cannot access Sway: Ensure that the correct email address was used and that the invitation was sent. Resend the invitation if necessary.

2. Permission changes not saving: Check your internet connection and ensure that you are logged in with the correct account. Try refreshing the page and reapplying the changes.

3. Unauthorized access: If someone gains access who shouldn't have, revoke their permissions immediately and review your sharing settings for potential security gaps.

6.3 Exporting and Printing Your Sway

6.3.1 Exporting to PDF

Exporting your Sway presentation to a PDF format can be incredibly useful for a variety of reasons. PDFs are widely accepted and used due to their portability and the fact that they preserve the formatting of the document across different devices and operating systems. Here, we'll walk through the detailed steps on how to export your Sway to PDF, along with tips and considerations to ensure your PDF output is of the highest quality.

Step-by-Step Guide to Exporting Your Sway to PDF

1. Open Your Sway:

   - Navigate to the Sway you want to export by logging into your Microsoft Sway account and selecting the specific Sway from your dashboard.

2. Preview Your Sway:

   - Before exporting, it's essential to preview your Sway to ensure everything is in place. Click the "Play" button at the top to see how your Sway looks in presentation mode. This will help you catch any errors or formatting issues that need correction before exporting.

3. Access the Export Options:

   - Once you're satisfied with your Sway, click on the "..." (More options) button at the top-right corner of the screen.

   - From the dropdown menu, select "Export" to open the export options.

4. Choose PDF Format:

   - In the export menu, you will see different format options. Select "PDF" to proceed with exporting your Sway as a PDF document.

5. Adjust Export Settings:

- Depending on the complexity and content of your Sway, you may have a few settings to adjust. These might include page size, orientation (portrait or landscape), and margins. Choose the settings that best fit your needs. For most presentations, the default settings should suffice.

6. Exporting Process:

- Click on "Export" or "Save as PDF". Your Sway will begin converting to a PDF file. This process may take a few moments depending on the length and content of your Sway.

7. Save the PDF:

- Once the export is complete, a prompt will appear allowing you to save the file. Choose a destination on your computer or cloud storage, and give your PDF a relevant name.

- Click "Save" to store the file in your desired location.

Tips for Ensuring a High-Quality PDF Export

1. Check Image Resolutions:

- Ensure all images in your Sway are of high resolution. Low-resolution images can appear pixelated in the PDF. Replace any low-quality images before exporting.

2. Consistent Formatting:

- Make sure your text formatting is consistent throughout the Sway. This includes font styles, sizes, and colors. Inconsistent formatting can look unprofessional in the PDF output.

3. Use Appropriate Page Breaks:

- While Sway is designed to be a fluid presentation tool, the PDF format is more rigid. If your Sway is lengthy, consider how content will be divided across pages. Manually insert page breaks in logical places to improve readability.

4. Check Interactive Elements:

- Interactive elements such as embedded videos and maps will not function in a static PDF. Ensure that the essential content is available in text or image form to retain the message without the interactive elements.

5. Proofread Thoroughly:

  - Perform a thorough proofread to catch any typos or errors. Once exported to PDF, making corrections can be more cumbersome.

Use Cases for Exporting Sway to PDF

- Offline Presentations:

  - If you need to present your Sway in a location with limited or no internet access, a PDF version allows you to maintain the integrity of your content without relying on a web connection.

- Printable Documents:

  - For conferences, meetings, or classrooms where printed materials are preferred, exporting to PDF provides a print-ready version of your Sway that can be easily distributed.

- Archiving:

  - PDFs are excellent for archiving purposes. They ensure that your content remains unchanged and accessible in the future, regardless of changes to software platforms.

- Sharing with Non-Technical Users:

  - Not everyone may be familiar with Sway or have access to it. PDF is a universally recognized format that can be opened on virtually any device, making it easier to share your work with a broader audience.

Troubleshooting Common Issues in PDF Export

1. Missing Images or Content:

  - If images or certain content elements are missing in the PDF, ensure they are properly uploaded and displayed in Sway. Re-export if necessary.

2. Poor Image Quality:

- Check the original resolution of your images. If the quality is poor, replace them with higher resolution versions before exporting.

3. Text Formatting Issues:

- Inconsistent fonts or sizes in the PDF often stem from the original Sway design. Double-check your Sway for any discrepancies and correct them prior to export.

4. Large File Size:

- High-resolution images and extensive content can result in a large PDF file. Consider compressing images before uploading them to Sway, or use PDF compression tools post-export to reduce file size.

By following these detailed steps and considerations, you can ensure that your Sway presentations are effectively exported to PDF, maintaining high quality and readability. This makes your presentations versatile and accessible in a variety of formats, enhancing your ability to communicate your ideas effectively.

6.3.2 Printing Options

Printing your Sway content can be beneficial for various reasons, such as creating physical copies for presentations, distributing handouts during meetings, or simply keeping a hard copy for your records. Although Sway is designed primarily for digital sharing and viewing, Microsoft provides a way to print your Sway content. This section will guide you through the steps involved in printing your Sway, exploring different methods and tips to ensure high-quality prints.

Understanding the Print Functionality in Sway

Before diving into the specifics of printing, it's essential to understand that Sway's design is inherently responsive and meant for digital consumption. This means that while you can print Sway content, the printed version might not fully capture the interactive and dynamic elements present in the digital format. However, with the right approach, you can still create a professional-looking printed document.

Steps to Print Your Sway

Here are the detailed steps to print your Sway:

1. Accessing the Print Option

To begin printing your Sway, follow these steps:

1. Open Your Sway: Start by opening the Sway you want to print. Make sure it is complete and formatted correctly.

2. Navigate to the Options Menu: In the top right corner of the Sway interface, click on the ellipsis (…) to open the options menu.

3. Select Export: From the dropdown menu, select "Export." This will give you options to export your Sway in different formats, typically PDF, which is suitable for printing.

2. Exporting to PDF

Since Sway does not have a direct print button, the recommended way to print your Sway content is by exporting it to PDF format first. Here's how you do it:

1. Choose Export to PDF: In the export options, select "Export to PDF." Sway will start converting your content into a PDF document.

2. Review the PDF: Once the export is complete, open the PDF file to review the content. Ensure that all text, images, and formatting appear as expected.

3. Adjust PDF Settings (if necessary): Sometimes, the PDF might need minor adjustments, such as tweaking margins or resizing images. You can use a PDF editor to make these changes before printing.

3. Printing the PDF

Now that you have your Sway content in a PDF format, you can proceed to print it:

1. Open the PDF in a PDF Reader: Use any standard PDF reader (such as Adobe Acrobat Reader) to open the exported PDF file.

2. Initiate the Print Command: Go to File > Print or simply press Ctrl + P (Cmd + P on Mac) to open the print dialog box.

3. Select Printer and Settings: Choose your printer from the list and adjust the print settings according to your needs. This includes selecting the number of copies, page range, color settings, and paper size.

4. Preview Before Printing: Always preview the document before printing to ensure everything looks good. This step helps you catch any potential issues, such as alignment problems or missing content.

5. Print the Document: Once you are satisfied with the preview, click on the Print button to start printing your Sway content.

Tips for High-Quality Prints

To ensure your printed Sway document looks professional and high-quality, consider the following tips:

1. Use High-Resolution Images

When creating your Sway, use high-resolution images to ensure they print clearly and without pixelation. Images with low resolution may look fine on screen but can appear blurry or grainy when printed.

2. Check Margins and Layout

Pay attention to margins and layout settings in both Sway and the PDF. Properly set margins ensure that no content is cut off during printing. Also, consider the layout (portrait or landscape) that best suits your content.

3. Color Settings

Ensure that your printer is set to print in color if your Sway includes colored elements. However, if you prefer a monochrome printout to save on ink or for a different aesthetic, adjust the printer settings accordingly.

4. Paper Quality

Choose the right type of paper for your print job. Higher-quality paper can make a significant difference in the appearance of your printed Sway, especially for presentations or professional handouts.

5. Test Print

If you are printing a large number of copies, it's a good idea to do a test print first. This allows you to check for any issues and make adjustments before printing the entire batch.

Alternative Printing Methods

Apart from exporting to PDF, you can use other methods to print your Sway content, depending on your specific needs and preferences:

1. Screenshot Method

For smaller sections or specific parts of your Sway, you can use the screenshot method:

1. Take Screenshots: Capture screenshots of the sections you want to print. Use screen capture tools like Snipping Tool (Windows) or Screenshot (Mac).

2. Compile in a Document: Insert these screenshots into a Word document or another text editor.

3. Format and Print: Format the document to ensure proper layout and print it as you would with any other document.

2. Browser Print

You can print your Sway directly from your browser, although this method may not offer the same level of control as exporting to PDF:

1. Open Sway in Browser: Open your Sway in a web browser.

2. Use Browser Print Function: Press Ctrl + P (Cmd + P on Mac) or go to the browser menu and select Print.

3. Adjust Print Settings: In the print dialog, adjust settings such as layout, margins, and scale.

4. Print the Page: Click Print to start printing directly from the browser.

Conclusion

Printing your Microsoft Sway content can be straightforward if you follow the right steps and pay attention to detail. By exporting to PDF and utilizing proper print settings, you can ensure that your printed Sway looks professional and high-quality. Whether you need printed copies for a presentation, meeting handouts, or personal records, the methods and tips provided in this section will help you achieve the best results. Remember, while Sway is designed for digital interaction, with careful preparation, you can still create impressive printed documents that capture the essence of your Sway content.

CHAPTER VII
Advanced Features and Tips

7.1 Utilizing Analytics

Analytics in Microsoft Sway provide valuable insights into how your audience interacts with your presentations. By understanding these analytics, you can refine your content to better engage viewers and achieve your presentation goals. This section will cover the fundamentals of accessing and interpreting Sway analytics.

7.1.1 Accessing Sway Analytics

Introduction to Sway Analytics

Sway analytics give you a window into your audience's behavior, including how they engage with your content, the time they spend on each section, and the overall reach of your Sway. Accessing these analytics is straightforward, but understanding them requires a bit of explanation. This guide will walk you through the steps to access and utilize Sway analytics effectively.

Step-by-Step Guide to Accessing Sway Analytics

1. Open Your Sway

  Start by logging into your Microsoft account and navigating to Sway. Open the specific Sway presentation for which you want to view analytics. This can be done from the dashboard where all your Sways are listed.

2. Access the Analytics Panel

Once your Sway is open, look for the menu or options button, usually represented by three dots (...) or a similar icon. Click on this to open a dropdown menu. From this menu, select "Analytics." This will open the analytics panel for your Sway.

3. Understanding the Dashboard

The analytics dashboard will present a variety of data points. Here are some key components you will encounter:

- Views: The total number of times your Sway has been viewed. This metric gives you a high-level overview of the reach of your presentation.

- Completion Rate: This shows the percentage of viewers who have viewed your Sway from start to finish. A high completion rate indicates that your content is engaging and holds the audience's attention.

- Average Viewing Time: The average amount of time viewers spend on your Sway. This can help you gauge the depth of engagement with your content.

- Engagement Insights: Detailed information about how viewers interact with different sections of your Sway, including clicks, scrolls, and time spent on each section.

Detailed Breakdown of Key Metrics

1. Views

Views represent the total number of times your Sway has been accessed. This is a straightforward metric but can be very telling. A high number of views indicates that your Sway is reaching a broad audience. However, it's essential to consider views in conjunction with other metrics, such as completion rate and average viewing time, to get a complete picture of engagement.

2. Completion Rate

The completion rate is crucial for understanding how engaging your content is. If you have a high number of views but a low completion rate, it might indicate that while your Sway is attracting interest, it may not be holding the audience's attention. To improve the completion rate, consider the following:

- Content Structure: Ensure your Sway is well-structured with a clear flow from beginning to end.

- Engaging Elements: Use interactive elements such as videos, images, and links to keep viewers engaged.

- Length of Content: Be concise. If your Sway is too long, viewers might lose interest before reaching the end.

3. Average Viewing Time

Average viewing time is another critical metric. It indicates how long, on average, viewers spend on your Sway. If this metric is low, it might suggest that viewers are quickly losing interest. To increase the average viewing time:

- Start Strong: Capture attention with a compelling introduction.

- Interactive Content: Incorporate interactive elements that require viewer interaction, such as embedded quizzes or clickable maps.

- Visual Appeal: Use high-quality images and a pleasing layout to make your Sway visually engaging.

4. Engagement Insights

Engagement insights provide a granular look at how viewers interact with different sections of your Sway. This includes:

- Clicks: Number of times interactive elements such as links or embedded content are clicked.

- Scroll Depth: How far down viewers scroll through your Sway.

- Time Spent on Sections: The amount of time viewers spend on specific sections.

These insights can help you identify which parts of your Sway are most engaging and which might need improvement. For example, if viewers are spending a lot of time on one section but quickly scrolling past another, you might need to enhance the content of the less engaging section.

Interpreting Sway Analytics

1. Identify Patterns

Look for patterns in your analytics data. Are there specific sections where viewers consistently drop off? Are there certain types of content that get more interaction? Identifying these patterns can help you understand what works and what doesn't.

2. Make Data-Driven Decisions

Use the insights gained from your analytics to make informed decisions about your content. For example, if you notice that interactive elements increase engagement, consider adding more interactive content to future Sways.

3. Iterate and Improve

Continuously iterate and improve your Sways based on the data you collect. Analytics should be an ongoing part of your content creation process, helping you refine and enhance your presentations over time.

Practical Tips for Using Sway Analytics

1. Set Clear Goals

Before delving into your analytics, set clear goals for what you want to achieve with your Sway. Are you aiming to increase overall views, improve the completion rate, or boost engagement with specific sections? Having clear goals will help you focus on the most relevant metrics.

2. Compare and Contrast

Compare the analytics of different Sways to understand what content performs best. This can help you replicate successful strategies and avoid repeating mistakes.

3. Engage with Your Audience

Use the insights from your analytics to engage with your audience. For example, if you notice that viewers are particularly interested in a specific topic, consider creating more content around that topic or expanding on it in future Sways.

Advanced Analytics Tools

While Sway provides built-in analytics, you might want to use more advanced tools for deeper insights. Consider integrating Sway with other analytics platforms such as Google Analytics. This can give you more detailed data and additional metrics to track.

Accessing Google Analytics for Sway

1. Set Up a Google Analytics Account

If you don't already have a Google Analytics account, set one up by visiting the Google Analytics website and following the instructions.

2. Get Your Tracking ID

Once your account is set up, you'll need a tracking ID. This ID will be used to link Google Analytics with your Sway.

3. Embed the Tracking Code

In Sway, go to the settings or options menu and look for an option to add custom HTML or a tracking code. Paste your Google Analytics tracking code here.

4. Monitor Your Data

After setting up the tracking code, monitor your data in Google Analytics. This platform offers more detailed insights, such as real-time user data, demographic information, and behavior flow.

Conclusion

Accessing and utilizing Sway analytics is crucial for creating effective and engaging presentations. By understanding and interpreting these analytics, you can make data-driven decisions that enhance your content and improve audience engagement. Remember, the key to success with analytics is continuous monitoring and iteration. Use the insights gained to refine your approach and create more compelling Sways that resonate with your audience.

7.1.2 Interpreting Data

Interpreting data within Microsoft Sway analytics is essential to understand how your content is performing and to make informed decisions for future presentations. This section will guide you through the key aspects of interpreting analytics data effectively.

1. Overview of Sway Analytics Data:

Microsoft Sway provides a comprehensive set of analytics that helps you track and understand how viewers interact with your Sway presentations. The data includes metrics such as views, unique visitors, average time spent on each Sway, and engagement rates. Each metric gives you valuable insights into your audience's behavior and preferences.

2. Key Metrics in Sway Analytics:

- Total Views: This metric indicates the total number of times your Sway has been viewed. A high number of views suggests that your content is attracting attention. However, it's important to look deeper into other metrics to understand the quality of engagement.

- Unique Visitors: This metric shows the number of distinct individuals who have viewed your Sway. Comparing unique visitors to total views can help you gauge how many people are returning to your content or if the same users are viewing it multiple times.

- Average Time Spent: This indicates the average amount of time viewers spend on your Sway. A longer average time suggests that your content is engaging and holding viewers' attention. Conversely, a shorter time may indicate that your content needs improvement to keep viewers interested.

- Engagement Rate: This measures how actively viewers are interacting with your Sway. Higher engagement rates mean viewers are not just passively reading but are interacting with embedded media, navigating through different sections, and engaging with the overall content.

3. Understanding Viewer Engagement:

- Heat Maps: Heat maps visually represent which sections of your Sway receive the most attention. Sections that are brightly colored on the heat map are where viewers spend the most time. Analyzing these maps can help you identify which parts of your content are most engaging and which may need improvement.

- Interaction Metrics: These metrics track how viewers interact with different elements within your Sway, such as clicking on links, playing videos, or viewing embedded content. High interaction rates on specific elements can indicate what types of content resonate most with your audience.

4. Analyzing Viewer Paths:

- Navigation Flow: This shows the path viewers take through your Sway. Understanding navigation flow can help you see if viewers are following your intended path or if they are skipping important sections. If many viewers are dropping off at a certain point, it might indicate that section needs to be more engaging or clearer.

- Drop-Off Points: Identifying where viewers tend to stop viewing your Sway can provide valuable insights. High drop-off rates in specific sections suggest that the content there might be less engaging or too complex. Revising these sections to make them more engaging or simplifying the information can help retain viewer interest.

5. Benchmarking and Comparing Data:

- Comparative Analysis: Comparing the performance of different Sways can help you identify trends and patterns. For instance, if one Sway consistently performs better than others, analyze its structure, content, and design to replicate its success in future presentations.

- Trend Analysis: Look for trends over time in your analytics data. Are your views increasing, decreasing, or staying consistent? Understanding these trends can help you determine if your content strategy is effective or if it needs adjustment.

6. Using Feedback for Improvement:

- Audience Feedback: Encouraging viewers to provide feedback can complement your analytics data. Direct feedback gives you qualitative insights that can explain why certain metrics are high or low. Incorporate viewer suggestions to make your Sways more effective.

- Iterative Improvement: Use your analytics data to make informed changes to your Sway. After making changes, compare the new data to previous performance to see if the adjustments had the desired effect. Continuous improvement based on data ensures that your content remains engaging and effective.

7. Practical Application of Analytics:

- Case Study 1: Improving Engagement: Suppose your analytics show that viewers spend a significant amount of time on the introduction but drop off quickly after that. This might indicate that your introduction is compelling, but the subsequent sections need to be more engaging. You can address this by adding interactive elements, multimedia, or breaking up long sections of text.

- Case Study 2: Enhancing Navigation: If the navigation flow data shows that viewers are not following the intended path and skipping key sections, you might need to improve the clarity and guidance within your Sway. Adding clear headings, navigational cues, and ensuring a logical flow can help guide viewers more effectively.

8. Utilizing Third-Party Tools:

While Sway provides built-in analytics, integrating third-party tools like Google Analytics can give you deeper insights. These tools offer advanced features such as custom reports, real-time data, and more detailed visitor segmentation. Combining data from Sway analytics and third-party tools can provide a more comprehensive understanding of your audience's behavior.

9. Reporting and Communicating Findings:

- Creating Reports: Use the analytics data to create detailed reports that summarize the performance of your Sway. Include key metrics, trends, and actionable insights. Visual aids like charts and graphs can make your reports more comprehensible and impactful.

- Communicating with Stakeholders: Share your findings with relevant stakeholders, such as team members, management, or clients. Highlight key successes and areas for improvement. Clear communication of analytics data helps in decision-making and demonstrates the value of your Sway presentations.

10. Continuous Learning and Adaptation:

- Staying Updated: Analytics tools and features evolve over time. Stay updated with the latest developments in Sway analytics and best practices in data interpretation.

- Learning from Others: Engage with the Sway community to learn from the experiences of other users. Sharing insights and learning from others can provide new perspectives and ideas for improving your Sways.

By effectively interpreting analytics data, you can enhance the impact of your Microsoft Sway presentations, making them more engaging and effective for your audience. Use the insights gained from analytics to continually refine and improve your content, ensuring it meets the needs and preferences of your viewers.

7.2 Accessibility Features

Microsoft Sway is designed to be an inclusive tool, ensuring that presentations and stories are accessible to a wide range of audiences, including those with disabilities. One critical aspect of accessibility is adding alternative text (alt text) to images and other media. Alt text provides a textual description of visual content, allowing screen readers to convey the information to users who are visually impaired. This section will guide you through the process of adding alt text to your Sway content, ensuring your presentations are accessible to all.

7.2.1 Adding Alt Text

What is Alt Text?

Alt text, or alternative text, is a brief description of an image or visual element embedded in a document or webpage. It serves several purposes:

1. Accessibility: Screen readers use alt text to describe images to visually impaired users, providing a richer and more inclusive experience.

2. SEO Benefits: Alt text helps search engines understand the content of images, improving search engine optimization (SEO).

3. Content Clarity: When images fail to load, alt text can provide context, ensuring that the message remains clear.

Why is Alt Text Important in Sway?

In Microsoft Sway, adding alt text is crucial because:

1. Inclusivity: It ensures that your content is accessible to everyone, including users with visual impairments.

2. Legal Compliance: Many regions have legal requirements for digital accessibility, including alt text for images.

3. Enhanced Communication: It helps in conveying the intended message clearly, even if the image does not load or is viewed by a user with a visual impairment.

Step-by-Step Guide to Adding Alt Text in Microsoft Sway

1. Open Your Sway Presentation

   - Navigate to the Sway you want to edit.

   - Click on the Sway to open it in the editing view.

2. Select the Image or Media

   - Locate the image or media element you want to add alt text to.

   - Click on the image to select it. You will see a toolbar or options related to the image appear.

3. Access the Alt Text Option

   - With the image selected, look for the "Details" or "Edit" option. This is usually represented by an icon resembling a pencil or text.

   - Click on this icon to open the media details pane.

4. Add Alt Text

   - In the media details pane, find the "Alt Text" or "Alternative Text" field.

   - Enter a concise and descriptive text that accurately describes the image. For example, if the image is of a dog playing in a park, your alt text might be "Golden retriever playing in a grassy park with a ball."

5. Save Changes

   - After entering the alt text, ensure you save your changes. This is typically done by clicking a "Save" or "Done" button.

   - Review the image to ensure the alt text has been added correctly.

Best Practices for Writing Alt Text

1. Be Descriptive and Concise:

   - Describe the content and function of the image. Avoid vague terms like "image" or "photo."

   - Keep it short but informative. Typically, a sentence or two is sufficient.

2. Focus on the Essential Information:

   - Include details that are important for understanding the context of the image in relation to the surrounding content.

   - Omit unnecessary information. For example, if an image is decorative and doesn't add meaning to the content, it might be appropriate to use empty alt text (alt="") to indicate that the image can be ignored by screen readers.

3. Consider the Context:

   - Write alt text that fits the context in which the image is used. The same image might need different alt text depending on the surrounding text and its purpose.

4. Avoid Redundancy:

   - Do not repeat information that is already provided in the text adjacent to the image.

   - Ensure that the alt text adds value and does not simply restate what is already clear from the context.

Examples of Good and Bad Alt Text

Example 1:

Image Description: A pie chart showing the market share of different smartphone brands.

- Bad Alt Text: "Pie chart."

- Good Alt Text: "Pie chart showing market share: Apple 40%, Samsung 30%, Huawei 20%, Others 10%."

Example 2:

Image Description: A photograph of a conference speaker on stage.

- Bad Alt Text: "Speaker."

- Good Alt Text: "Speaker John Doe presenting at the 2024 Tech Innovations Conference."

Advanced Tips for Alt Text

1. Complex Images:

   - For charts, graphs, and complex diagrams, consider providing a brief overview in the alt text and a more detailed description in the surrounding text or a separate description section.

2. Decorative Images:

   - If an image is purely decorative and does not convey any meaning or information, use an empty alt attribute (alt="") to indicate that it can be ignored by assistive technologies.

3. Functional Images:

   - For images that act as links or buttons, describe the function rather than the appearance. For example, "Submit button" or "Link to the homepage."

Testing and Reviewing Alt Text

1. Use a Screen Reader:

   - Test your Sway presentation using a screen reader to ensure that the alt text is being read correctly and provides meaningful descriptions.

   - Popular screen readers include NVDA (NonVisual Desktop Access) and JAWS (Job Access With Speech).

2. Seek Feedback:

   - Get feedback from users who rely on screen readers to ensure that your alt text descriptions are helpful and appropriate.

   - Incorporate suggestions to improve the accessibility of your Sway presentations.

3. Regular Updates:

   - Review and update alt text regularly, especially when making changes to the content or design of your Sway.

   - Ensure that new images and media elements added to your presentation also include appropriate alt text.

Conclusion

Adding alt text to images and media in Microsoft Sway is a simple yet powerful way to make your presentations accessible to a broader audience. By following the steps and best practices outlined in this section, you can ensure that your content is inclusive, informative, and compliant with accessibility standards. Remember, effective alt text enhances the user experience for everyone, making your Sway presentations more engaging and impactful.

7.2.2 Using High Contrast Mode

High contrast mode is an essential accessibility feature that enhances the usability of Microsoft Sway for individuals with visual impairments, particularly those who have difficulty distinguishing between colors or reading text with low contrast. High contrast mode changes the visual design of the interface to use a color scheme with a higher degree of contrast between foreground and background elements. This makes text and other visual elements stand out more clearly.

In this section, we will guide you through the process of enabling and customizing high contrast mode in Microsoft Sway, and provide tips on optimizing your content to be more accessible for all users.

Understanding High Contrast Mode

High contrast mode alters the appearance of the Sway interface to make it easier for users with visual impairments to read and navigate. This mode typically involves using dark backgrounds with light text or vice versa. It minimizes the use of color gradients and focuses on solid colors that are easier to differentiate.

Why Use High Contrast Mode?

1. Enhanced Readability: Text becomes more legible due to the increased contrast between text and background.

2. Reduced Eye Strain: Users who struggle with low-contrast themes can use high contrast mode to reduce eye strain, making it more comfortable to view content for extended periods.

3. Accessibility Compliance: Utilizing high contrast mode helps in meeting accessibility standards, ensuring your content is inclusive and accessible to all users.

Enabling High Contrast Mode in Microsoft Sway

To enable high contrast mode in Microsoft Sway, follow these steps:

Step 1: Access Microsoft Sway

1. Open your web browser and go to the [Microsoft Sway](https://sway.office.com) website.

2. Log in with your Microsoft account credentials.

Step 2: Open a Sway or Create a New One

1. From the Sway dashboard, select an existing Sway to edit or click "Create New" to start a new project.

Step 3: Access the Accessibility Settings

1. In the top-right corner of the Sway interface, click on the gear icon to open the "Settings" menu.

2. From the drop-down menu, select "Accessibility View."

Step 4: Enable High Contrast Mode

1. Once in the accessibility view, look for the "High Contrast" toggle switch.

2. Click on the switch to enable high contrast mode. The interface will immediately change to a high contrast color scheme.

Customizing High Contrast Mode

While Microsoft Sway does not offer extensive customization options for high contrast mode within the application itself, you can make adjustments to the overall display settings on your operating system to further enhance the high contrast experience. Here's how to customize high contrast settings on Windows and macOS:

Customizing High Contrast Mode on Windows

1. Open Settings:

  - Press `Windows + I` to open the Settings app.

2. Navigate to Ease of Access:

  - In the Settings app, select "Ease of Access."

3. Enable High Contrast:

  - From the Ease of Access menu, select "High Contrast."

  - Toggle the switch to "On" to enable high contrast mode.

4. Customize High Contrast Theme:

  - Under the "Choose a theme" section, select a high contrast theme that suits your needs.

  - You can further customize the theme by clicking on "Edit" and changing the colors for text, hyperlinks, disabled text, selected text, and button text.

  - Once you've made your adjustments, click "Apply."

Customizing High Contrast Mode on macOS

1. Open System Preferences:

   - Click on the Apple menu and select "System Preferences."

2. Navigate to Accessibility:

   - In System Preferences, select "Accessibility."

3. Enable High Contrast:

   - In the Accessibility menu, select "Display."

   - Check the box next to "Increase contrast" to enable a higher contrast display.

4. Additional Adjustments:

   - You can also enable "Reduce transparency" to further improve visibility by removing transparent effects.

   - Adjust the display contrast slider to fine-tune the level of contrast to your preference.

Optimizing Your Sway Content for High Contrast Mode

Enabling high contrast mode is just the first step in making your Sway presentations accessible. It's equally important to design your content with accessibility in mind. Here are some tips to optimize your Sway content for high contrast mode:

 1. Use Clear and Simple Language

- Write in plain language to ensure that your content is easily understandable.

- Avoid jargon and complex sentences that might be difficult for some users to comprehend.

 2. Choose Accessible Color Combinations

- Ensure that the colors you use for text and backgrounds have sufficient contrast. Use tools like the [WebAIM Color Contrast Checker](https://webaim.org/resources/contrastchecker/) to verify color contrast ratios.

- Avoid using color alone to convey information. Use text labels, patterns, or icons to supplement color coding.

3. Use Descriptive Headings and Labels

- Organize your content with clear headings and subheadings to improve navigation.

- Use descriptive labels for links and buttons to help users understand their purpose without needing additional context.

4. Provide Alt Text for Images

- Add descriptive alt text to all images to ensure that screen reader users can understand the content.

- Be concise but descriptive, focusing on the essential information conveyed by the image.

5. Avoid Automatic Content Changes

- Avoid using animations or automatic content changes that could be distracting or disorienting for users with visual impairments.

- If animations are necessary, provide controls for users to pause or stop the animations.

Testing Your Sway in High Contrast Mode

After enabling high contrast mode and optimizing your content, it's crucial to test your Sway to ensure that it is fully accessible. Here are some steps for testing your Sway in high contrast mode:

Step 1: Enable High Contrast Mode

Follow the steps outlined earlier to enable high contrast mode in Microsoft Sway or your operating system.

Step 2: Review Your Content

1. Text Visibility:

  - Ensure that all text is clearly visible and readable.

  - Check for any instances where text blends into the background.

2. Image Clarity:

   - Verify that images are still clear and meaningful.

   - Check that alt text is correctly associated with each image.

3. Navigation:

   - Test the navigation elements, such as links and buttons, to ensure they are easy to identify and use.

   - Ensure that users can navigate through the Sway using keyboard shortcuts and screen readers.

4. Interactive Elements:

   - Test any interactive elements, such as embedded videos or forms, to ensure they function correctly in high contrast mode.

Collecting Feedback

To further improve the accessibility of your Sway presentations, consider collecting feedback from users who rely on high contrast mode. Here are some ways to gather useful feedback:

1. User Testing:

   - Conduct user testing sessions with individuals who have visual impairments.

   - Observe how they interact with your Sway and ask for their feedback on the usability and readability of the content.

2. Surveys:

   - Create surveys to gather feedback from a broader audience.

   - Ask specific questions about the effectiveness of high contrast mode and any challenges users faced.

3. Accessibility Audits:

- Perform accessibility audits using tools like [WAVE](https://wave.webaim.org/) or [AXE](https://www.deque.com/axe/).

- Identify any issues and make necessary adjustments to improve accessibility.

Conclusion

Using high contrast mode in Microsoft Sway is a powerful way to make your presentations more accessible to individuals with visual impairments. By following the steps outlined in this section, you can enable high contrast mode, customize it to meet your needs, and optimize your content to ensure it is inclusive and accessible.

Remember, accessibility is not just about following guidelines; it's about creating a user experience that is welcoming and usable for everyone. By taking the time to understand and implement accessibility features like high contrast mode, you are making a positive impact on the lives of all your users.

7.3 Tips and Tricks for Effective Sways

7.3.1 Engaging Your Audience

Engaging your audience is crucial for the success of any presentation. Microsoft Sway offers a variety of features and techniques that can help you capture and maintain your audience's attention. This section will guide you through these features and provide detailed tips and tricks to make your Sways more engaging and interactive.

1. Understand Your Audience

Before you start creating your Sway, it's essential to understand your audience. Knowing their interests, preferences, and level of familiarity with the topic will help you tailor your content effectively.

- Audience Analysis: Identify who your audience is. Are they students, professionals, or a general audience? Understanding their background will help you choose the right tone and content.

- Audience Interests: What are the main interests of your audience? Highlighting these interests in your Sway will keep them engaged.

- Prior Knowledge: Assess the level of prior knowledge your audience has about the topic. This will help you decide how much background information you need to provide.

2. Create a Compelling Narrative

A compelling narrative can make your presentation more interesting and memorable. Sway allows you to create a story-like flow that keeps your audience engaged.

- Introduction: Start with a strong introduction that captures attention. This could be an interesting fact, a question, or a brief story.

- Flow: Ensure your content flows logically from one section to the next. Use headings and subheadings to guide your audience through the narrative.

- Conclusion: End with a strong conclusion that summarizes the key points and leaves a lasting impression.

3. Use High-Quality Visuals

Visual content is a powerful tool for engagement. Sway makes it easy to incorporate a variety of visual elements into your presentation.

- Images: Use high-quality, relevant images to complement your text. Images can help illustrate your points and make your Sway more visually appealing.

- Videos: Embed videos to provide dynamic content. Videos can explain complex topics more effectively than text alone.

- Infographics: Create and include infographics to present data in an engaging and easy-to-understand format.

4. Incorporate Interactive Elements

Interactive elements can make your Sway more engaging by encouraging audience participation.

- Interactive Charts: Use interactive charts to allow your audience to explore data in more depth.

- Embedded Content: Embed content such as maps, social media posts, and other web content to provide a richer experience.

- Forms and Quizzes: Incorporate forms and quizzes to engage your audience actively. This can also provide you with valuable feedback.

5. Keep Your Content Concise

Long blocks of text can be overwhelming and disengaging. Keep your content concise and to the point.

- Bullet Points: Use bullet points to break down information into easily digestible chunks.

- Short Paragraphs: Keep paragraphs short and focused on a single idea.

- Clear Language: Use clear and straightforward language to ensure your audience understands your message.

6. Utilize Sway's Design Features

Sway offers various design features that can enhance the visual appeal of your presentation.

- Design Themes: Choose a design theme that matches the tone of your presentation. Sway provides a range of themes to choose from.

- Custom Colors and Fonts: Customize colors and fonts to align with your branding or to create a specific mood.

- Layout Options: Experiment with different layout options to find the one that best presents your content.

7. Add Personal Touches

Adding personal touches can make your Sway more relatable and engaging.

- Personal Stories: Share personal stories or anecdotes related to your topic. This can make your presentation more interesting and memorable.

- Personal Photos: Include personal photos where appropriate to add a human element to your Sway.

8. Practice Good Design Principles

Good design principles can enhance the readability and overall impact of your Sway.

- White Space: Use white space effectively to avoid clutter and improve readability.

- Alignment: Ensure elements are properly aligned to create a clean and professional look.

- Contrast: Use contrast to highlight important elements and improve visibility.

9. Test Your Sway

Testing your Sway before presenting it to your audience can help you identify and fix any issues.

- Preview Mode: Use Sway's preview mode to see how your presentation will look to your audience.

- Feedback: Share your Sway with a few trusted individuals and ask for their feedback. Use their insights to make improvements.

- Revisions: Be prepared to make revisions based on feedback and your own observations.

10. Engage with Your Audience During the Presentation

Engaging with your audience during the presentation can keep them interested and involved.

- Questions: Encourage your audience to ask questions. This can lead to a more interactive and engaging presentation.

- Polls: Use polls to gather opinions and make your audience feel involved.

- Live Demonstrations: If applicable, include live demonstrations to show your content in action.

11. Follow Up After the Presentation

Engagement doesn't end when the presentation does. Following up with your audience can leave a lasting impression and encourage further interaction.

- Q&A Sessions: Hold a Q&A session after the presentation to address any remaining questions.

- Follow-Up Materials: Provide follow-up materials such as handouts or additional resources.

- Feedback Requests: Ask for feedback on your presentation to understand what worked well and what could be improved.

12. Continuous Improvement

Finally, always look for ways to improve your presentations. Keep learning and experimenting with new techniques.

- Stay Updated: Keep up with the latest features and updates in Microsoft Sway.

- Learn from Others: Study other effective Sways to see what techniques they use.

- Experiment: Don't be afraid to experiment with new ideas and formats.

By following these tips and tricks, you can create engaging and effective presentations with Microsoft Sway. Remember, the key to engagement is to know your audience, tell a compelling story, use high-quality visuals, and incorporate interactive elements. Keep your content concise, practice good design principles, and always look for ways to improve. With these strategies, you'll be able to captivate your audience and make your presentations stand out.

7.3.2 Streamlining Your Workflow

Creating a dynamic and engaging presentation with Microsoft Sway can be an enjoyable and efficient process, especially when you leverage various tips and tricks to streamline your workflow. In this section, we will explore detailed strategies and techniques that can help you optimize your time and effort, allowing you to produce high-quality Sways with minimal hassle.

1. Plan Your Content

Before diving into Sway, take some time to plan your content. Outline the main points you want to cover and organize them into a logical sequence. This can save you time during the creation process and ensure that your Sway has a clear and coherent structure.

- Create an Outline: Start with a basic outline that includes the key sections and subtopics of your presentation. This helps you stay focused and ensures you don't miss any important points.

- Gather Resources: Collect all the images, videos, and other media you plan to include. Having everything ready in advance can significantly speed up the process.

2. Use Templates and Themes

Microsoft Sway offers a variety of templates and themes that can provide a professional look with minimal effort. These pre-designed templates can save you time and help you maintain a consistent aesthetic throughout your presentation.

- Choosing the Right Template: Select a template that aligns with the tone and purpose of your presentation. For instance, a business template might be suitable for corporate presentations, while an education template could be perfect for classroom use.

- Customizing Themes: While templates offer a great starting point, you can further customize the themes to better suit your content. Adjust colors, fonts, and layouts to match your brand or personal style.

3. Leverage the Power of the Storyline

The Storyline in Sway is a powerful tool that helps you organize and manage your content efficiently. By mastering the use of the Storyline, you can streamline your workflow and create more engaging presentations.

- Drag and Drop: The drag-and-drop feature allows you to quickly rearrange sections and cards. This flexibility makes it easy to adjust your content as you go.

- Grouping Cards: Group related cards together to create sections within your Sway. This not only makes your presentation easier to navigate but also helps you manage your content more effectively.

4. Utilize Keyboard Shortcuts

Keyboard shortcuts can save you a significant amount of time, especially when performing repetitive tasks. Familiarize yourself with common shortcuts to enhance your efficiency.

- Common Shortcuts: Learn shortcuts for basic actions like copying (Ctrl + C), pasting (Ctrl + V), and undoing changes (Ctrl + Z). These can quickly become second nature and speed up your workflow.

- Sway-Specific Shortcuts: Explore Sway-specific shortcuts such as adding new cards, duplicating cards, and navigating between sections.

5. Integrate with Other Microsoft Tools

One of the advantages of using Microsoft Sway is its seamless integration with other Microsoft Office tools. Leveraging these integrations can simplify your workflow and enhance your presentations.

- Embedding Office Documents: Easily embed Word documents, Excel spreadsheets, and PowerPoint slides directly into your Sway. This allows you to present detailed information without having to recreate it.

- OneDrive Integration: Store your media files in OneDrive for easy access and sharing. You can directly insert files from your OneDrive into Sway, saving time and ensuring consistency.

6. Automate Repetitive Tasks

Automation can greatly reduce the time spent on repetitive tasks, allowing you to focus on more important aspects of your presentation.

- Using the Remix Feature: The Remix button in Sway can automatically apply a new design to your presentation. This can be a quick way to refresh the look of your Sway without manually adjusting each element.

- Custom Scripts: If you have specific formatting or design requirements, consider creating custom scripts or using third-party tools that can automate these processes.

7. Collaborate Effectively

Collaborating with others can enhance the quality of your Sway, but it can also introduce complexities. By using Sway's collaboration features effectively, you can streamline the process and ensure smooth teamwork.

- Inviting Collaborators: Use Sway's sharing options to invite collaborators. Set appropriate permissions to control what others can edit.

- Real-Time Collaboration: Work simultaneously with team members in real-time. This can help speed up the creation process and ensure that everyone's contributions are integrated smoothly.

- Comments and Feedback: Utilize the comments feature to gather feedback from collaborators. This can help you make necessary adjustments and improvements more efficiently.

8. Optimize Media Usage

High-quality media can make your Sway more engaging, but it can also increase the file size and slow down loading times. Optimize your media usage to strike a balance between quality and performance.

- Compressing Images: Use image compression tools to reduce the file size of your images without compromising quality. This can help your Sway load faster and improve the overall user experience.

- Using Online Media: Instead of uploading large video files, consider embedding videos from platforms like YouTube or Vimeo. This reduces the file size of your Sway and leverages the hosting capabilities of these platforms.

- Alt Text for Accessibility: Always add alt text to your images and media. This not only improves accessibility but also helps search engines understand the content of your Sway.

9. Regularly Save and Backup Your Work

Ensuring that your work is saved and backed up can prevent data loss and save you from having to redo work.

- Auto-Save Feature: Sway automatically saves your work, but it's good practice to manually save your progress at key milestones.

- Version Control: Keep track of different versions of your Sway. This can be useful if you need to revert to a previous version or compare changes.

10. Seek Feedback and Iterate

Creating an effective Sway is often an iterative process. Seek feedback from peers, mentors, or your target audience and use their insights to refine your presentation.

- Pilot Testing: Before finalizing your Sway, conduct a pilot test with a small audience. Gather their feedback on the content, design, and overall effectiveness.

- Continuous Improvement: Based on the feedback, make necessary adjustments and improvements. Remember that the best presentations often go through several iterations before reaching their final form.

11. Stay Updated with Sway Features

Microsoft regularly updates Sway with new features and improvements. Staying updated with these changes can help you leverage the latest tools and functionalities.

- Following Updates: Keep an eye on the official Microsoft Sway blog or community forums for announcements about new features and updates.

- Experimenting with New Tools: Don't hesitate to experiment with new tools and features. They might offer more efficient ways to achieve your goals or enhance your presentations.

Conclusion

Streamlining your workflow in Microsoft Sway involves a combination of planning, utilizing built-in tools and features, and staying organized. By following these tips and tricks, you can create professional and engaging presentations more efficiently. Whether you're a beginner or an experienced user, these strategies can help you make the most out of Sway and ensure that your presentations are both effective and visually appealing.

CHAPTER VIII
Use Cases for Microsoft Sway

8.1 Educational Uses

8.1.1 Creating Interactive Lessons

Creating interactive lessons with Microsoft Sway offers a dynamic and engaging way to present educational content. Sway's unique features allow educators to create visually appealing and interactive lessons that can enhance student learning and participation. This section will provide a detailed guide on how to create interactive lessons using Microsoft Sway.

Step 1: Planning Your Lesson

Before diving into Sway, it is essential to plan your lesson. Consider the following:

- Objective: What is the goal of the lesson? What should students learn by the end of it?

- Content: What topics will be covered? What materials (text, images, videos) will you need?

- Structure: How will the lesson be organized? What is the logical flow of information?

Step 2: Setting Up Your Sway

1. Access Microsoft Sway: Go to sway.office.com and sign in with your Microsoft account.

2. Create a New Sway: Click on "Create New" to start a new Sway project.

Step 3: Adding Content to Your Sway

1. Title Your Sway: Begin by giving your Sway a title that reflects the lesson's topic.

2. Add a Title Card: The first card is usually the title card. Click on it and type in the lesson title.

Step 4: Organizing Your Lesson Content

1. Introduction: Introduce the lesson with a brief overview. Use a text card to write a short introduction. You can add images or videos to make it more engaging.

2. Main Content: Break down the lesson into sections or topics. For each section, use a combination of text, images, videos, and other media to explain the concepts.

  - Text Cards: Use text cards for explanations, definitions, and key points.

  - Image Cards: Add images to illustrate concepts or provide visual aids.

  - Video Cards: Embed videos to offer additional explanations or real-world examples.

  - Embed Content: Use the embed option to include interactive content like quizzes or external resources.

Step 5: Making Your Lesson Interactive

1. Add Interactive Elements: Incorporate interactive elements to keep students engaged.

  - Group Cards: Use group cards to combine multiple media types in one section. For example, you can group text, images, and videos together to provide a comprehensive view of a topic.

  - Stack Cards: Use stack cards for step-by-step instructions or to present multiple images in a slideshow format.

  - Comparison Cards: Use comparison cards to compare two images or concepts side by side.

2. Incorporate Assessments: Use Sway's interactive features to add quizzes or polls to assess student understanding.

- Embed Quizzes: Create quizzes using tools like Microsoft Forms or Google Forms and embed them into your Sway.

- Polls and Surveys: Use embedded polls or surveys to gather student feedback or check for understanding.

Step 6: Designing Your Sway

1. Choose a Design Theme: Click on "Design" in the menu to choose a design theme. Sway offers various themes that you can customize to match the tone and style of your lesson.

2. Customize Your Layout: Adjust the layout settings to organize your content effectively. You can choose between vertical, horizontal, or slide-based layouts.

Step 7: Reviewing and Sharing Your Lesson

1. Preview Your Sway: Click on "Play" to preview your Sway. Make sure all content is in place and interactive elements work correctly.

2. Share Your Sway: Once satisfied, share your Sway with your students. Click on "Share" and choose your preferred sharing method. You can share a link, embed the Sway on a website, or invite specific people to view it.

Step 8: Engaging Students with Interactive Lessons

1. Encourage Participation: During the lesson, encourage students to interact with the content. Ask them to explore embedded media, participate in quizzes, and engage with interactive elements.

2. Facilitate Discussions: Use the interactive features to spark discussions. For example, after a video or quiz, ask students to share their thoughts or answers.

3. Monitor Progress: Use embedded quizzes and assessments to monitor student progress and understanding. Provide feedback based on their responses.

Step 9: Enhancing Your Lessons with Advanced Features

1. Use Analytics: Sway provides analytics to track how students interact with your lesson. Use this data to understand which parts of the lesson are most engaging and which may need improvement.

2. Update and Improve: Based on feedback and analytics, continuously update and improve your lessons. Add new content, refine interactive elements, and adjust the layout as needed.

Example: Interactive History Lesson

To illustrate the process, let's create an interactive history lesson on the American Revolution.

1. Title Card: "The American Revolution: An Interactive Lesson"

2. Introduction: A brief overview of the American Revolution, including its significance and key events.

3. Main Content:

  - Section 1: Causes of the Revolution

    - Text explaining the causes

    - Images of historical documents

    - Embedded video of a documentary

  - Section 2: Key Events

    - Timeline of key events using stack cards

    - Comparison card to compare British and American perspectives

  - Section 3: Important Figures

    - Text and images of key figures like George Washington and King George III

    - Embedded video interviews with historians

- Section 4: Outcomes and Impact

  - Text explaining the outcomes

  - Embedded quiz to assess understanding

4. Interactive Elements:

  - Group card combining text, images, and videos

  - Embedded quiz created with Microsoft Forms

  - Poll asking students about their opinions on the revolution's impact

5. Design and Layout:

  - Choose a historical theme

  - Customize the layout to a vertical format for easy scrolling

6. Review and Share:

  - Preview the Sway to ensure all elements work

  - Share the Sway link with students

7. Engagement and Monitoring:

  - Encourage students to explore the content and participate in quizzes

  - Facilitate a discussion based on the quiz results and poll responses

By following these steps, educators can create interactive and engaging lessons with Microsoft Sway. This approach not only enhances the learning experience but also allows for more dynamic and flexible teaching methods.

8.1.2 Student Projects and Portfolios

Microsoft Sway is a powerful tool for students to create dynamic, engaging projects and portfolios. It offers a versatile platform that allows students to showcase their work in an interactive and visually appealing manner. In this section, we will explore how students can utilize Sway for their projects and portfolios, providing detailed guidance on each step to ensure they make the most out of this tool.

Introduction to Student Projects and Portfolios in Sway

Student projects and portfolios are essential components of the educational process, enabling learners to present their research, findings, and achievements. Traditional methods of creating projects often involve static documents or presentations. However, with Microsoft Sway, students can create interactive and multimedia-rich presentations that can be easily shared and viewed on any device. This not only enhances the presentation quality but also engages the audience more effectively.

Getting Started with Sway

1. Creating a New Sway:

   - Log in to your Microsoft account and navigate to the Sway homepage.

   - Click on "Create New" to start a new Sway project. You can choose to start from a blank canvas or use a template.

   - Give your Sway a title that reflects the theme of your project or portfolio.

2. Setting Up Your Storyline:

   - The storyline is the backbone of your Sway where you add and organize content.

   - Begin by outlining the sections of your project or portfolio. For example, if you are creating a portfolio, you might have sections like "Introduction," "Academic Achievements," "Extracurricular Activities," and "Future Goals."

   - Add headings to your storyline to structure your content.

Adding Content to Your Project or Portfolio

1. Text and Narration:

   - Add text cards to provide detailed explanations, descriptions, and narrations.

   - Use headings, subheadings, and bullet points to organize text and make it easy to read.

   - Highlight key points and use formatting options like bold, italics, and underline to emphasize important information.

2. Incorporating Images:

   - Upload images related to your project or achievements. For a portfolio, include photos of certificates, events, or projects.

   - Use the "Image" card to add individual images or create an image gallery to showcase multiple photos.

   - Add captions to your images to provide context and explain their relevance.

3. Embedding Videos:

   - Videos can enhance your Sway by providing visual and auditory elements.

   - Use the "Video" card to upload your own videos or embed videos from platforms like YouTube or Vimeo.

   - Ensure your videos are high quality and relevant to the content. For example, include a video presentation of a project or a recording of an event you participated in.

4. Adding Links and Documents:

   - Use the "Embed" card to add links to external resources, websites, or online documents.

   - Include links to articles, research papers, or other online content that supports your project.

   - Embed documents like PDFs or Word files to provide additional information or references.

Customizing the Design and Layout

1. Choosing a Theme:

  - Sway offers a variety of themes that can be applied to your project to enhance its visual appeal.

  - Choose a theme that matches the tone and purpose of your project. For example, a professional theme for academic projects or a colorful theme for creative portfolios.

2. Adjusting Layouts:

  - Use the "Design" tab to adjust the layout of your Sway. You can choose between vertical, horizontal, or grid layouts.

  - Experiment with different layouts to see which one best presents your content.

3. Using Grouping and Emphasis:

  - Group related content together to create a cohesive flow. For example, group images and text that pertain to a specific project or achievement.

  - Use the "Emphasis" option to highlight important sections or content. This can draw attention to key parts of your project.

Sharing and Collaboration

1. Sharing Your Sway:

  - Once you have completed your Sway, it's time to share it with your audience.

  - Click on the "Share" button and choose your sharing settings. You can share your Sway with specific people or generate a link that can be viewed by anyone.

  - Ensure you adjust the permissions accordingly, especially if you are sharing sensitive or personal information.

2. Collaborating with Peers:

  - Sway allows you to collaborate with others in real-time.

  - Invite classmates or teachers to view or edit your Sway by sending them an invitation link.

- Collaborate effectively by assigning different sections or tasks to each team member and ensuring everyone contributes their part.

Tips for Creating Effective Student Projects and Portfolios

1. Be Clear and Concise:

   - Ensure your content is clear and to the point. Avoid unnecessary jargon or overly complex sentences.

   - Focus on delivering your message effectively and concisely.

2. Use High-Quality Media:

   - High-quality images and videos enhance the overall presentation and make your Sway more engaging.

   - Avoid using blurry or low-resolution media as it can detract from the professionalism of your project.

3. Keep the Audience in Mind:

   - Consider who will be viewing your Sway and tailor your content accordingly.

   - For academic projects, ensure you provide enough detail and supporting evidence. For portfolios, highlight your achievements and skills prominently.

4. Review and Edit:

   - Before sharing your Sway, review it thoroughly for any errors or inconsistencies.

   - Edit your content for clarity, grammar, and punctuation to ensure it is polished and professional.

5. Stay Organized:

   - Maintain a logical flow in your Sway to guide the audience through your content smoothly.

   - Use headings and subheadings to break down sections and make navigation easier.

Examples of Student Projects and Portfolios

1. Science Fair Project:

   - Create a Sway to document your science fair project, including the hypothesis, research, methodology, results, and conclusion.

   - Include images of your experiments, charts of your data, and videos of your presentations.

2. Art Portfolio:

   - Showcase your art pieces in a Sway portfolio. Include images of your artwork, descriptions of the techniques used, and the inspiration behind each piece.

   - Embed videos of your creative process or exhibitions you participated in.

3. Class Assignment:

   - Use Sway to present a class assignment, such as a book report or research paper.

   - Combine text, images, and videos to create an engaging and interactive presentation.

4. Extracurricular Activities Portfolio:

   - Document your participation in extracurricular activities like sports, music, or clubs.

   - Include images and videos of events, awards, and achievements, along with descriptions of your roles and experiences.

Conclusion

Microsoft Sway offers a versatile and user-friendly platform for students to create impressive projects and portfolios. By leveraging its interactive features, multimedia capabilities, and collaborative tools, students can present their work in a compelling and professional manner. Whether for academic purposes or personal achievements, Sway helps students to effectively communicate their ideas and accomplishments to their audience.

8.2 Business Applications

8.2.1 Marketing Presentations

WelcomeSure! Below is a detailed guide on using Microsoft Sway for creating Marketing Presentations.

Chapter 8: Use Cases for Microsoft Sway

8.2 Business Applications

8.2.1 Marketing Presentations

Creating effective marketing presentations is crucial for conveying the value and benefits of products or services to potential customers. Microsoft Sway offers a dynamic platform for developing visually appealing and interactive marketing presentations. This section provides a detailed guide on how to use Sway for marketing presentations, including planning, content creation, design customization, and sharing.

1. Planning Your Marketing Presentation

Before diving into Sway, it's essential to plan your marketing presentation. Consider the following steps:

a. Define Your Goals:

Identify the primary objectives of your presentation. Are you introducing a new product, showcasing features, or persuading an audience to take action? Clear goals will guide your content creation.

b. Know Your Audience:

Understand who your audience is and what they care about. Tailor your message to resonate with their needs and interests.

c. Structure Your Content:

Organize your presentation into clear sections. A typical structure might include an introduction, problem statement, solution, benefits, case studies, and a call to action.

2. Starting Your Marketing Presentation in Sway

With your plan in place, it's time to start creating your presentation in Sway:

a. Create a New Sway:

Log into your Microsoft account and open Sway. Click on "Create New" to start a fresh presentation.

b. Choose a Template:

Sway offers various templates that can serve as a starting point for your marketing presentation. Select a template that aligns with your brand's aesthetic or the presentation's theme.

3. Adding Content to Your Sway

Content is the core of your marketing presentation. Sway allows you to add diverse types of content seamlessly:

a. Text Content:

  - Titles and Headings: Use clear and compelling titles and headings to guide your audience through the presentation.

  - Body Text: Keep your text concise and focused. Highlight key points and use bullet points for readability.

  - Call to Action: Include a strong call to action (CTA) at the end of your presentation to encourage the desired response from your audience.

b. Visual Content:

  - Images: Add high-quality images that complement your message. Sway allows you to upload images from your device or search for online images directly within the platform.

  - Videos: Embed videos to demonstrate product features, customer testimonials, or promotional clips. You can add videos from YouTube, Vimeo, or upload your own.

  - Charts and Graphs: Use charts and graphs to visualize data and statistics. This can make complex information more digestible.

c. Interactive Content:

  - Embeds: Embed content from other websites, such as social media posts, Google Maps, or interactive widgets. This can add depth and engagement to your presentation.

- Links: Add hyperlinks to direct your audience to additional resources, product pages, or contact forms.

4. Customizing the Design of Your Marketing Presentation

A well-designed presentation enhances the impact of your message. Microsoft Sway offers various customization options:

a. Design Themes:

 - Select a Theme: Choose a design theme that matches your brand's visual identity. Sway provides several built-in themes, each with unique color schemes and fonts.

 - Customize Colors and Fonts: If the pre-made themes don't fully match your brand, customize the colors and fonts to align with your brand guidelines.

b. Layout Options:

 - Vertical vs. Horizontal Layout: Decide whether you want your presentation to scroll vertically or horizontally. Vertical layouts are suitable for linear storytelling, while horizontal layouts can create a more dynamic experience.

 - Grouping and Alignment: Group related content together and align elements for a clean and organized look. Sway's intuitive drag-and-drop interface makes it easy to arrange your content.

c. Using the Remix Feature:

 - Automatic Design Suggestions: The Remix feature allows Sway to automatically suggest different design layouts based on your content. This can provide inspiration and help you discover new design possibilities.

5. Enhancing Engagement with Interactive Elements

Engagement is key in marketing presentations. Sway offers interactive features that can captivate your audience:

a. Interactive Charts and Graphs:

  - Data Visualizations: Use interactive charts and graphs to present data in an engaging way. Allow your audience to explore the data by interacting with the visual elements.

b. Embedded Forms and Surveys:

  - Feedback and Interaction: Embed forms and surveys to collect feedback from your audience. This can provide valuable insights and foster interaction.

c. Interactive Timelines and Storylines:

  - Dynamic Storytelling: Use interactive timelines and storylines to create a narrative flow. This can guide your audience through the presentation in an engaging manner.

6. Sharing and Presenting Your Sway

Once your marketing presentation is complete, it's time to share it with your audience:

a. Sharing Settings:

  - Shareable Link: Generate a shareable link to distribute your presentation. You can control the privacy settings to determine who can view or edit the Sway.

- Embed Code: Embed your Sway on websites, blogs, or social media platforms using the provided embed code.

b. Presenting Live:

- Live Presentation Mode: Use Sway's live presentation mode to present directly from the platform. This mode optimizes your Sway for viewing on large screens and during live sessions.

- Presenter Notes: Add presenter notes to guide you through the presentation. These notes are visible only to you and can help keep your presentation smooth and organized.

c. Exporting Your Sway:

- Export to PDF: Export your Sway to PDF for offline sharing or printing. This can be useful for providing handouts or archiving your presentation.

7. Best Practices for Effective Marketing Presentations

Creating an effective marketing presentation involves more than just using the right tools. Here are some best practices to keep in mind:

a. Keep It Concise:

- Avoid Information Overload: Focus on key messages and avoid overwhelming your audience with too much information. Use visuals and concise text to convey your points.

b. Tell a Story:

- Narrative Flow: Structure your presentation as a story. Start with a compelling introduction, build up to the main points, and conclude with a strong call to action.

c. Use High-Quality Visuals:

 - Professional Imagery: Use high-resolution images and professional-quality videos. Visuals should enhance your message, not distract from it.

d. Engage Your Audience:

 - Interactive Elements: Incorporate interactive elements to keep your audience engaged. Ask questions, include polls, and encourage participation.

e. Practice and Rehearse:

 - Smooth Delivery: Practice your presentation to ensure a smooth delivery. Rehearse with colleagues or friends to get feedback and refine your approach.

Conclusion

Microsoft Sway is a powerful tool for creating impactful marketing presentations. Its flexibility and interactive features allow you to craft presentations that not only convey your message effectively but also engage and inspire your audience. By following this guide, you can leverage Sway's capabilities to create professional and persuasive marketing presentations that stand out.

Remember, the key to a successful marketing presentation is to combine clear and compelling content with visually appealing design. Use the tools and features available in Sway to their fullest potential, and you'll be well on your way to creating presentations that leave a lasting impression.

8.2.2 Internal Reports

Introduction to Internal Reports in Microsoft Sway

Internal reports are essential for any organization to communicate information efficiently across different departments and teams. Microsoft Sway offers a dynamic platform to create visually appealing, interactive, and engaging internal reports that can be easily shared and updated. Whether you are reporting on quarterly results, project updates, or operational metrics, Sway can help you present your data in a compelling way.

Getting Started with Internal Reports in Sway

Step 1: Define the Purpose and Audience of Your Report

Before you start creating your internal report, it's crucial to define the purpose and audience. Are you reporting financial results to the executive team, providing a project update to stakeholders, or sharing department performance metrics? Understanding the purpose and audience will guide the structure and content of your report.

Step 2: Gather Your Data and Materials

Collect all the necessary data, charts, images, and other materials that you will include in your report. This might involve exporting data from other software, taking screenshots, or preparing visual aids such as graphs and infographics.

Step 3: Start a New Sway

Log in to your Microsoft account and open Sway. Click on "Create New" to start a blank Sway. Alternatively, you can use one of the available templates if you find one that closely matches your needs.

Structuring Your Internal Report

Step 4: Create the Report Title and Introduction

Your report should start with a clear title and an introduction that outlines the purpose and scope of the report. Use a Title Card to add the report's title and a Text Card for the introduction.

Example:

- Title Card: "Q1 Financial Performance Report"

- Text Card: "This report provides an overview of our financial performance for the first quarter of 2024. It includes key metrics, performance highlights, and areas for improvement."

Step 5: Add a Table of Contents

To help your audience navigate through the report, add a Table of Contents. This can be created using a combination of Text Cards and links to different sections within the Sway.

Example:

- Text Card: "Table of Contents"

  - Introduction

  - Executive Summary

  - Financial Metrics

  - Departmental Performance

  - Project Updates

  - Conclusion

 Adding Content to Your Report

Step 6: Executive Summary

Provide a high-level overview of the report's key findings and recommendations. This section should be concise and to the point.

Example:

- Text Card: "Executive Summary"

 - "The first quarter of 2024 has shown a 10% increase in revenue compared to Q1 2023. However, operational costs have risen by 5%, impacting our net profit margin. Key projects are on track, but there are areas where efficiency improvements are needed."

Step 7: Financial Metrics

Present detailed financial metrics such as revenue, expenses, profit margins, and any other relevant data. Use a combination of Text Cards, Image Cards (for charts and graphs), and Embed Cards (to include dynamic content such as interactive charts from Excel).

Example:

- Text Card: "Financial Metrics"

- Image Card: Insert charts and graphs showing revenue and expenses

- Embed Card: Embed an interactive Excel chart showing monthly performance

Step 8: Departmental Performance

Detail the performance of different departments. This section can be broken down into subsections for each department. Use Text Cards for descriptions and Image Cards for visual aids.

Example:

- Text Card: "Departmental Performance"

 - "Sales Department: The sales team achieved 120% of their Q1 targets, driven by new client acquisitions."

 - "Marketing Department: Marketing campaigns generated a 15% increase in lead generation, but conversion rates need improvement."

Step 9: Project Updates

Provide updates on key projects. Each project update should include the project name, current status, milestones achieved, and any challenges or next steps.

Example:

- Text Card: "Project Updates"

 - "Project A: Completed Phase 1 ahead of schedule. Phase 2 is on track for completion by Q2."

 - "Project B: Encountered delays due to resource constraints. Mitigation plan in place to address issues."

Step 10: Conclusion and Recommendations

Summarize the report's findings and provide recommendations for the next steps. This section should reinforce the key points and suggest actionable steps based on the report's data.

Example:

- Text Card: "Conclusion and Recommendations"

 - "In conclusion, while Q1 performance shows positive revenue growth, cost management needs to be addressed to improve profitability. It is recommended to implement cost-saving measures and enhance operational efficiency."

Customizing the Design and Layout

Step 11: Choose a Design Theme

Select a design theme that aligns with your organization's branding and the nature of the report. Click on the "Design" tab and choose a theme that complements your content.

Step 12: Customize the Layout

Adjust the layout to ensure the report is visually appealing and easy to navigate. Use the "Layout" options to switch between vertical and horizontal scrolling, and group related content together for better flow.

Sharing and Collaborating

Step 13: Share Your Report

Once your report is complete, it's time to share it with your audience. Click on the "Share" button and choose your sharing options. You can generate a shareable link, invite collaborators, or even embed the Sway in an email or website.

Step 14: Collaborate with Team Members

If you need input from other team members, invite them to collaborate on the Sway. Set permissions to allow them to edit or view the report as needed. Collaboration ensures that the report is accurate and includes insights from relevant stakeholders.

Step 15: Exporting and Printing

If a physical copy of the report is required, export your Sway to PDF. Go to the "..." menu, select "Export," and choose "PDF." Ensure that the layout and formatting are preserved in the exported document for a professional appearance.

Tips and Best Practices

Engage Your Audience:

- Use multimedia elements like videos, images, and interactive charts to keep your audience engaged.

- Highlight key metrics and insights to ensure they stand out.

Maintain Consistency:

- Stick to a consistent design theme and formatting throughout the report.

- Use headings and subheadings to organize content and make it easy to follow.

Update Regularly:

- Regularly update the report with the latest data and insights.

- Notify your audience when significant updates are made to ensure they are always informed.

Utilize Analytics:

- Use Sway's analytics feature to track how your audience interacts with the report.

- Adjust your content and presentation based on the insights gained from analytics.

By following these steps, you can create effective and engaging internal reports using Microsoft Sway. This tool not only simplifies the process of creating reports but also enhances the way information is communicated within your organization.

8.3 Personal Uses

8.3.1 Family Newsletters

Creating family newsletters with Microsoft Sway can be a delightful way to keep family members updated about events, milestones, and special moments. Sway's user-friendly interface and versatile design options make it easy to produce visually appealing and interactive newsletters. This section will guide you through the process of creating a family newsletter using Microsoft Sway, from planning and content creation to design and sharing.

Step 1: Planning Your Family Newsletter

Before diving into Sway, it's important to plan the content and structure of your newsletter. Consider the following aspects:

1. Purpose and Audience: Determine the primary goal of your newsletter. Are you updating family members about recent events, celebrating milestones, or sharing plans for future gatherings? Understanding your purpose will help you decide the content and tone. Your audience is likely to be family members of various ages, so ensure the content is inclusive and engaging for everyone.

2. Content Outline: Sketch an outline of the topics you want to include. Common sections in a family newsletter might include:

  - Family news and updates

  - Upcoming events

  - Spotlight on family members (e.g., birthdays, achievements)

  - Photo galleries

  - Personal messages or anecdotes

3. Frequency: Decide how often you want to publish your newsletter. Monthly, quarterly, or annual newsletters are common choices. Consistency helps family members look forward to the updates.

Step 2: Setting Up Your Sway

1. Access Microsoft Sway: Open your web browser and navigate to sway.office.com. Sign in with your Microsoft account. If you don't have an account, you'll need to create one.

2. Create a New Sway: Click on the "Create New" button. You'll be prompted to choose between starting from a blank canvas or using a template. For a family newsletter, you might find it useful to start with a template designed for newsletters.

Step 3: Adding Content to Your Newsletter

1. Title and Introduction:

   - Title Card: Click on the title card to add the title of your newsletter. This should be catchy and reflective of the content. For example, "The Johnson Family Times – Summer Edition 2024."

   - Introduction Card: Add a brief introduction welcoming readers and giving an overview of what to expect in this edition. This sets the tone and provides context.

2. Family News and Updates:

   - Text Card: Use text cards to add updates about family members. Highlight significant events such as weddings, graduations, or new job opportunities. For each update, include a brief description and relevant details.

   - Image Card: Enhance the updates with images. You can upload photos directly from your device or search for images online. Personal photos make the newsletter more engaging and relatable.

3. Upcoming Events:

- Text Card: List upcoming family events such as reunions, holiday gatherings, or planned trips. Include dates, locations, and any important information.

- Embed Calendar: If you have a family calendar, consider embedding it in the Sway. This allows family members to view and synchronize event dates easily.

4. Spotlight on Family Members:

- Group Cards: Group cards are great for spotlight sections. You can create a card for each family member being highlighted. Include their photo, name, and a brief write-up about their recent achievements or special moments.

- Text and Image Cards: Combine text and image cards to create a rich, multimedia experience. For example, if celebrating a child's graduation, include a photo of the graduation ceremony and a note about their future plans.

5. Photo Galleries:

- Image Gallery Card: Add an image gallery to showcase a collection of photos. This could be a highlight reel from a recent family vacation, a birthday party, or any other memorable event.

- Descriptions: Include brief descriptions for each photo to provide context and make the gallery more informative and engaging.

6. Personal Messages or Anecdotes:

- Text Card: Reserve a section for personal messages from family members. This could include holiday greetings, thank you notes, or funny anecdotes.

- Embed Audio: If you want to add a personal touch, consider embedding audio messages. Family members can record messages and share them, adding a layer of warmth and connection to the newsletter.

Step 4: Customizing the Design

1. Design Themes:

- Choosing a Theme: Click on the "Design" tab at the top of the screen. Browse through the available themes and select one that suits the tone and style of your newsletter. Themes control the overall look and feel, including fonts, colors, and background images.

- Customizing the Theme: You can further customize the selected theme by adjusting the color scheme, fonts, and layout. This allows you to create a unique design that reflects your family's personality.

2. Layout Options:

- Vertical, Horizontal, or Slideshow: Sway offers different layout options. Vertical layouts are great for newsletters, as they mimic the format of a traditional document. However, horizontal and slideshow layouts can also be effective, depending on your content and design preferences.

- Grouping and Ordering Cards: Organize your cards in a logical sequence. You can group related cards together and move them around to ensure a smooth flow of information.

3. Background Images and Colors:

- Background Images: You can set a background image for your Sway. Choose an image that complements the theme and enhances the visual appeal without overwhelming the content.

- Colors: Adjust the color palette to ensure text is readable and the overall design is visually appealing. Stick to a cohesive color scheme that matches your family's style or the season (e.g., warm colors for a summer edition).

Step 5: Reviewing and Previewing Your Sway

1. Preview Mode: Click on the "Preview" button to see how your newsletter will appear to readers. This allows you to experience the Sway from a reader's perspective and identify any areas that need adjustment.

- Interactive Elements: Test any interactive elements, such as embedded calendars or audio messages, to ensure they function correctly.

- Content Flow: Ensure the content flows logically and is easy to navigate. Make any necessary adjustments to the order or grouping of cards.

2. Proofreading: Carefully proofread your newsletter for any spelling or grammatical errors. Clear and error-free content enhances the professionalism and readability of your newsletter.

Step 6: Sharing Your Family Newsletter

1. Share Settings:

  - Sharing Options: Click on the "Share" button. You'll be presented with various sharing options. You can share your Sway via a link, email, or social media.

  - Privacy Settings: Adjust the privacy settings to control who can view your Sway. For family newsletters, you might want to restrict access to specific people by requiring a password or limiting access to those with the link.

2. Generating a Shareable Link:

  - Copy Link: Generate a shareable link and copy it. You can then paste this link into an email or a family group chat.

  - Email Sharing: Sway allows you to send the newsletter directly via email. Enter the email addresses of your family members and include a personal message if desired.

3. Embedding Sway:

  - Embed Code: If you have a family website or blog, consider embedding your Sway directly onto the site. This provides easy access for family members who frequently visit the site.

4. Social Media Sharing:

  - Social Platforms: Share your newsletter on family social media groups or pages. Sway provides built-in options to share on platforms like Facebook, Twitter, and LinkedIn.

Step 7: Gathering Feedback and Improving Future Editions

1. Collecting Feedback:

- Surveys and Polls: Consider including a survey or poll link in your newsletter to gather feedback from family members. Ask for their opinions on the content, design, and any suggestions for future editions.

- Email Replies: Encourage family members to reply to the newsletter email with their thoughts and suggestions.

2. Implementing Changes:

- Review Feedback: Review the feedback received and identify common themes or suggestions. Use this information to make improvements in future editions.

- Continuous Improvement: Strive to improve each edition of your family newsletter. Incorporate new features, design elements, and content ideas to keep it fresh and engaging.

Creating a family newsletter with Microsoft Sway is a wonderful way to stay connected with loved ones. By following these detailed steps, you can produce a visually appealing, interactive, and engaging newsletter that your family will look forward to receiving. Happy Swaying.

8.3.2 Event Planning

Planning an event, whether it's a wedding, birthday party, corporate function, or community gathering, requires careful organization and effective communication. Microsoft Sway offers a powerful and flexible platform to streamline event planning and create visually appealing, interactive content that can be easily shared with attendees. This section will guide you through the process of using Microsoft Sway for event planning, from initial setup to final presentation.

Getting Started with Event Planning in Sway

1. Define the Purpose and Scope of the Event

Before diving into Sway, it's essential to have a clear understanding of your event's purpose and scope. This includes the event's goals, target audience, budget, and timeline. Outline these elements in a document or spreadsheet, as this information will guide the creation of your Sway presentation.

2. Choose a Sway Template

Microsoft Sway offers various templates that can be customized for event planning. To start a new Sway, log in to your Microsoft account, navigate to Sway, and choose a template that best fits your event. For event planning, templates like "Event Announcement" or "Newsletter" can serve as a good starting point.

3. Customize the Sway Title and Cover Image

The title and cover image set the tone for your Sway. Choose a title that reflects the essence of your event and an engaging cover image. The cover image can be a photo related to the event or a custom graphic that captures the event's theme.

Creating the Event Overview

1. Event Details

Create a section that provides an overview of the event. This should include:

- Event Name

- Date and Time

- Location

- Event Description

Use text cards for this information. For example:

Event Name: Annual Company Retreat

Date and Time: September 15, 2024, from 9:00 AM to 5:00 PM

Location: Mountain View Resort, 1234 Retreat Lane, Springfield

Event Description: Join us for a day of team-building activities, workshops, and relaxation at the beautiful Mountain View Resort. This event is designed to foster collaboration, creativity, and rejuvenation among our employees.

2. Agenda

Detail the event agenda to give attendees a clear understanding of what to expect. Use a combination of text and media cards to make the agenda visually appealing. For example:

Agenda:

- 9:00 AM - Welcome and Breakfast

- 10:00 AM - Team Building Activities

- 12:00 PM - Lunch

- 1:00 PM - Workshop: Innovation in the Workplace

- 3:00 PM - Free Time and Networking

- 5:00 PM - Closing Remarks

Consider adding images or icons next to each agenda item to make it more engaging.

Invitations and RSVPs

1. Creating Invitations

Design a visually appealing invitation within Sway. Include all the essential details and add interactive elements such as maps and links to RSVP forms. For example, you can embed a Google Map showing the event location or a link to an online registration form.

2. Sharing the Invitation

Once your invitation is ready, use Sway's sharing options to distribute it. You can generate a shareable link, email the invitation directly from Sway, or post it on social media platforms. Ensure that the invitation is accessible to all potential attendees.

Managing Event Information

1. Speaker and Guest Profiles

If your event features speakers or special guests, create profiles for them within your Sway. Use text and media cards to highlight their backgrounds, expertise, and what attendees can expect from their sessions. This adds a personal touch and helps attendees connect with the speakers.

2. Venue Information

Provide detailed information about the event venue. Include maps, photos, and descriptions of the location. Highlight important areas such as parking, entrances, and registration desks. For example:

Venue: Mountain View Resort

Parking: Free parking is available at the venue.

Entrances: Main entrance is located on Retreat Lane, with additional entrances on the north side of the resort.

Registration Desk: Located in the main lobby, open from 8:00 AM.

Interactive Features and Media

1. Embedding Multimedia

Enhance your Sway with multimedia content. Embed videos, photo galleries, and audio clips to make the presentation more dynamic. For instance, include a welcome video from the event organizer or a slideshow of previous events to build excitement.

2. Interactive Elements

Add interactive elements such as polls, surveys, and quizzes. This not only engages attendees but also provides valuable feedback. For example, include a pre-event survey to understand attendees' expectations or a quiz related to the event's theme.

Finalizing and Sharing Your Sway

1. Previewing and Testing

Before sharing your Sway, preview it to ensure that all elements are displayed correctly and that the content flows logically. Test all links and interactive features to ensure they work as intended.

2. Sharing Options

Microsoft Sway offers multiple sharing options. You can share your Sway via:

- Link: Generate a shareable link that can be sent via email or posted on social media.

- Embed: Embed the Sway on your website or blog.

- Export: Export your Sway as a PDF for offline viewing or printing.

Choose the method that best suits your audience and distribution strategy.

Post-Event Follow-Up

1. Sharing Event Highlights

After the event, update your Sway with highlights such as photos, videos, and key takeaways. Share this updated Sway with attendees as a recap of the event. For example:

Event Highlights:

- Photo Gallery: A collection of photos from the event.

- Video Recap: A short video summarizing the day's activities.

- Key Takeaways: Highlights from the workshop and team-building sessions.

2. Gathering Feedback

Include a section for post-event feedback. Use a survey or feedback form embedded in your Sway to collect attendees' thoughts and suggestions. This information is invaluable for planning future events.

3. Thank You Message

End your Sway with a thank you message to all attendees, speakers, and organizers. Acknowledge their participation and contributions to the event's success. For example:

Thank You: We extend our heartfelt thanks to everyone who attended and contributed to the success of the Annual Company Retreat. Your participation made this event truly special. We look forward to seeing you at future events.

Conclusion

Using Microsoft Sway for event planning not only simplifies the process but also enhances the overall experience for attendees. Its interactive features, ease of use, and seamless sharing capabilities make it an ideal tool for creating engaging and visually appealing event presentations. Whether you're planning a small gathering or a large conference, Sway can help you organize and present your event details in a professional and captivating manner.

CHAPTER IX
Troubleshooting and Support

9.1 Common Issues and Solutions

9.1.1 Connectivity Problems

Connectivity issues can be one of the most frustrating problems when working with Microsoft Sway, as they can disrupt your workflow, cause delays, and prevent you from accessing or sharing your Sway presentations. This section provides a comprehensive guide to troubleshooting and resolving connectivity problems to ensure a smooth experience with Microsoft Sway.

Understanding Connectivity Problems

Connectivity problems with Microsoft Sway can manifest in various ways, including:

- Inability to access the Sway website: You might be unable to load the Sway website or log into your account.

- Failed uploads: Images, videos, or other media might fail to upload.

- Sync issues: Changes made to a Sway might not save or sync correctly.

- Sharing issues: You might face difficulties sharing your Sway with others or generating shareable links.

These issues can stem from various causes, including network problems, browser settings, or issues with Microsoft's servers. The following steps provide detailed instructions on how to diagnose and resolve these problems.

Step-by-Step Troubleshooting Guide

1. Check Your Internet Connection

Before delving into more specific troubleshooting steps, ensure that your internet connection is stable and functioning correctly.

1. Verify Connectivity: Check if other websites are loading properly. If other sites are slow or not loading, the issue might be with your internet connection.

2. Restart Your Router: Sometimes, restarting your router can resolve connectivity issues. Unplug the router, wait for 30 seconds, and plug it back in.

3. Use a Wired Connection: If you're using Wi-Fi, try switching to a wired connection to see if it improves stability.

2. Clear Browser Cache and Cookies

Your browser's cache and cookies can sometimes cause connectivity issues with web applications like Microsoft Sway.

1. Clear Cache and Cookies:

  - In Google Chrome: Click on the three-dot menu > More tools > Clear browsing data. Select "All time" for the time range, check "Cookies and other site data" and "Cached images and files," and click "Clear data."

  - In Mozilla Firefox: Click on the three-bar menu > Options > Privacy & Security. Under "Cookies and Site Data," click "Clear Data," check both boxes, and click "Clear."

  - In Microsoft Edge: Click on the three-dot menu > Settings > Privacy, search, and services. Under "Clear browsing data," click "Choose what to clear," check "Cookies and other site data" and "Cached images and files," and click "Clear now."

2. Restart Browser: Close and reopen your browser after clearing the cache and cookies.

3. Update Your Browser

Using an outdated browser can lead to compatibility issues with Microsoft Sway.

1. Check for Updates:

- In Google Chrome: Click on the three-dot menu > Help > About Google Chrome. The browser will check for updates and install them automatically.

- In Mozilla Firefox: Click on the three-bar menu > Help > About Firefox. The browser will check for updates and install them automatically.

- In Microsoft Edge: Click on the three-dot menu > Help and feedback > About Microsoft Edge. The browser will check for updates and install them automatically.

2. Restart Browser: Close and reopen your browser after updating.

4. Disable Browser Extensions

Certain browser extensions can interfere with the functionality of Microsoft Sway.

1. Disable Extensions:

- In Google Chrome: Click on the three-dot menu > More tools > Extensions. Toggle off each extension.

- In Mozilla Firefox: Click on the three-bar menu > Add-ons and themes > Extensions. Toggle off each extension.

- In Microsoft Edge: Click on the three-dot menu > Extensions. Toggle off each extension.

2. Test Sway: After disabling extensions, try accessing Sway again. If the issue is resolved, enable extensions one by one to identify the problematic extension.

5. Check for Network Restrictions

Network restrictions, such as firewalls or proxy settings, can block access to Microsoft Sway.

1. Check Firewall Settings:

- On Windows: Go to Settings > Update & Security > Windows Security > Firewall & network protection. Ensure that your firewall isn't blocking Sway.

- On Mac: Go to System Preferences > Security & Privacy > Firewall. Ensure that your firewall isn't blocking Sway.

2. Proxy Settings:

- On Windows: Go to Settings > Network & Internet > Proxy. Ensure that your proxy settings aren't blocking Sway.

- On Mac: Go to System Preferences > Network > Advanced > Proxies. Ensure that your proxy settings aren't blocking Sway.

6. Test on a Different Network

If possible, try accessing Microsoft Sway on a different network, such as a mobile hotspot or a friend's Wi-Fi, to determine if the issue is specific to your network.

1. Switch Networks: Connect to a different Wi-Fi network or use a mobile hotspot.

2. Test Sway: Try accessing Sway again to see if the issue persists.

7. Contact Your Internet Service Provider (ISP)

If none of the above steps resolve the issue, contact your ISP to check if there are any known issues or restrictions that might be affecting your connectivity.

1. Call ISP Support: Explain the connectivity issue and ask if there are any known problems or restrictions.

2. Follow ISP Instructions: Follow any troubleshooting steps provided by your ISP.

8. Check Microsoft Service Status

Sometimes, connectivity issues can be due to problems with Microsoft's servers.

1. Check Service Status:

- Visit the [Microsoft Service Health](https://status.office.com/) page to check if there are any reported issues with Sway.

2. Wait for Resolution: If there are service issues, wait for Microsoft to resolve them.

Conclusion

Connectivity problems can significantly impact your experience with Microsoft Sway, but most issues can be resolved with systematic troubleshooting. By following the steps outlined above, you can diagnose and fix common connectivity problems, ensuring a smooth and uninterrupted workflow. If problems persist despite these efforts, reaching out to Microsoft Support or your ISP may provide additional solutions.

By maintaining a stable internet connection and keeping your browser and network settings optimized, you can minimize the likelihood of encountering connectivity issues in the future, allowing you to fully leverage the capabilities of Microsoft Sway.

9.1.2 Media Playback Issues

Media playback issues in Microsoft Sway can be frustrating, especially when you are trying to create a seamless and engaging presentation. This section will cover common media playback problems users might encounter and provide detailed solutions to resolve them.

Understanding Media Playback Issues

Media playback issues can arise from a variety of factors, including file compatibility, internet connectivity, browser settings, and device performance. These issues can manifest in different ways, such as videos not playing, audio not being heard, or images not loading correctly. Addressing these problems requires a systematic approach to identify the root cause and apply the appropriate fix.

Common Media Playback Problems and Their Solutions

1. Video Playback Issues

  - Problem: Video Not Playing

    - Possible Causes:

      - Unsupported video format

      - Internet connectivity issues

      - Browser compatibility problems

- Solutions:

- Check Video Format: Ensure that the video format is supported by Sway. Common supported formats include MP4, WMV, and MOV. If the video is in a different format, consider converting it to a supported format using a video converter tool.

- Improve Internet Connectivity: Ensure that you have a stable internet connection. Try playing the video on a different network or using a wired connection to see if the issue persists.

- Update or Change Browser: Make sure your browser is up to date. Sway works best with modern browsers such as Microsoft Edge, Google Chrome, or Mozilla Firefox. If you encounter issues, try using a different browser.

- Problem: Video Buffering or Lagging

- Possible Causes:

- Slow internet speed

- Large video file size

- Solutions:

- Reduce File Size: Consider compressing the video file to reduce its size. This can help improve playback performance. There are various online tools and software available to compress video files without significantly reducing quality.

- Improve Internet Speed: If possible, upgrade to a faster internet plan. Additionally, closing other bandwidth-consuming applications or devices on your network can help.

- Problem: Video Quality Issues

- Possible Causes:

- Low-resolution video file

- Playback settings

- Solutions:

- Upload High-Resolution Videos: Ensure that you are uploading videos with a resolution that meets your presentation needs. For most purposes, 720p or 1080p resolution is sufficient.

- Adjust Playback Settings: Some browsers or devices may have settings that affect video quality. Check and adjust these settings to ensure optimal playback.

2. Audio Playback Issues

 - Problem: No Sound in Video or Audio Files

  - Possible Causes:

   - Muted browser or device

   - Audio file issues

  - Solutions:

- Check Mute Settings: Ensure that your device and browser are not muted. Check the volume settings on your computer and within the browser.

- Verify Audio File: Make sure the audio file is not corrupted. Try playing the audio file in a different media player to confirm it works correctly.

 - Problem: Audio Out of Sync with Video

  - Possible Causes:

   - Encoding issues

   - Large file size

  - Solutions:

- Re-encode Video: Use video editing software to re-encode the video and ensure that the audio is properly synced. Tools like HandBrake or Adobe Premiere can help with this process.

- Compress File: Similar to video buffering issues, reducing the file size can help improve synchronization.

3. Image Display Issues

   - Problem: Images Not Loading

     - Possible Causes:

       - Unsupported image format

       - Large image file size

       - Browser settings

     - Solutions:

     - Check Image Format: Ensure that the images are in a supported format such as JPEG, PNG, or GIF. Convert any unsupported formats to one of these.

     - Reduce File Size: Compress large images to reduce their file size. This can improve loading times. Online tools like TinyPNG or Photoshop can assist with image compression.

     - Adjust Browser Settings: Ensure that your browser is set to display images. Some privacy or security settings may block images from loading. Check the settings and adjust accordingly.

4. Embedding Media Issues

   - Problem: Embedded Media Not Displaying

     - Possible Causes:

       - Incorrect embed code

       - Restrictions on the source website

     - Solutions:

     - Verify Embed Code: Double-check the embed code for any errors. Ensure that it is correctly copied and pasted into Sway.

     - Check Source Restrictions: Some websites restrict embedding of their content. Ensure that the source allows embedding. If not, consider linking to the media instead of embedding it.

5. General Troubleshooting Steps

  - Clear Browser Cache: Clearing the browser cache can resolve many playback issues caused by outdated or corrupted data. This can be done through the browser settings.

  - Update Software: Ensure that your operating system, browser, and any plugins are up to date. Updates often include bug fixes and performance improvements.

  - Try a Different Device: If playback issues persist, try accessing Sway on a different device. This can help determine if the issue is device-specific.

  - Disable Extensions: Some browser extensions can interfere with media playback. Temporarily disable extensions to see if this resolves the issue.

 Preventive Measures for Smooth Media Playback

To avoid media playback issues in the future, consider the following preventive measures:

1. Use Compatible Media Formats: Always use media formats that are known to be compatible with Microsoft Sway. Stick to common formats like MP4 for videos, MP3 for audio, and JPEG/PNG for images.

2. Optimize Media Files: Before uploading, optimize your media files by compressing them and ensuring they are of appropriate resolution and quality. This can prevent many playback issues and improve overall performance.

3. Regularly Update Software: Keep your browser and operating system up to date to benefit from the latest improvements and bug fixes. Enable automatic updates if possible.

4. Test Media on Multiple Devices: Before finalizing your Sway presentation, test the media playback on multiple devices and browsers to ensure compatibility and performance.

5. Use Reliable Internet Connections: For critical presentations, ensure that you have a reliable and fast internet connection. Consider having a backup connection available as well.

6. Provide Alternative Access: If embedding media is problematic, provide alternative access methods such as direct links to the media files. This ensures that your audience can still access the content even if playback issues occur.

Conclusion

Media playback issues can disrupt the flow and impact of your Microsoft Sway presentations. By understanding the common problems and applying the solutions outlined in this guide, you can troubleshoot and resolve these issues effectively. Implementing preventive measures will also help ensure smooth media playback in your future Sway projects, enhancing the overall experience for your audience.

9.2 Accessing Microsoft Support

9.2.1 Online Resources

When encountering issues with Microsoft Sway, leveraging online resources can be an effective way to find solutions. Microsoft provides a plethora of online resources designed to help users troubleshoot problems, learn new features, and get the most out of their Sway experience. Here, we'll explore some of the key online resources available and how to use them effectively.

Microsoft Support Website

The Microsoft Support website is the primary resource for finding official solutions to problems with Sway. Here's how to navigate and utilize this site:

1. Visit the Microsoft Support Website: Open your browser and go to support.microsoft.com. This is the hub for all official support resources provided by Microsoft.

2. Search for Sway: Use the search bar at the top of the page and type "Microsoft Sway". This will bring up a list of articles, guides, and troubleshooting steps specifically related to Sway.

3. Browse the Categories: You can refine your search by categories such as "Getting Started", "Troubleshooting", "Account Management", and "Feature Guides". This helps in narrowing down the resources to the most relevant ones.

4. Read Official Articles: The search results will include articles that provide step-by-step instructions, screenshots, and videos. These official articles are thoroughly vetted and reliable sources of information.

5. Utilize the Knowledge Base: The Knowledge Base is a repository of articles that address common issues, explain features, and provide tips and tricks. Look for articles that match the specific issue you're facing.

Microsoft Community Forums

The Microsoft Community Forums are another excellent resource where you can interact with other users and Microsoft support personnel:

1. Access the Community Forums: Navigate to the [Microsoft Community](https://answers.microsoft.com).

2. Select Sway as the Product: From the product list, choose "Sway". This filters the questions and discussions to those specifically about Sway.

3. Search for Similar Issues: Before posting a new question, use the search bar to see if someone else has already asked about the same issue. This can save time as the solution might already be available.

4. Ask the Community: If you don't find a solution, you can post a new question. Provide detailed information about the issue, including what steps you've already taken to try and resolve it. This helps community members and Microsoft staff give you more accurate advice.

5. Respond to Replies: Engage with those who respond to your question. They might ask for additional details or suggest troubleshooting steps. Following up promptly can lead to a quicker resolution.

Microsoft Sway Help Center

The Sway Help Center is a dedicated section on the Sway website that offers help and guidance:

1. Visit the Sway Help Center: Go to sway.com/help.

2. Explore the Topics: The Help Center is organized into topics such as "Create and Edit", "Share and Collaborate", and "Manage and Organize". These categories make it easy to find relevant help articles.

3. Watch Tutorial Videos: The Help Center often includes tutorial videos that visually demonstrate how to use different features of Sway. These can be particularly helpful if you prefer learning through visual aids.

4. Use the FAQ Section: The Frequently Asked Questions (FAQ) section addresses common queries and issues. It's a quick way to get answers to standard questions without having to delve deeply into articles.

Online Tutorials and Courses

Various online platforms offer tutorials and courses on using Microsoft Sway. These range from free YouTube videos to comprehensive courses on educational websites like Udemy, LinkedIn Learning, and Coursera:

1. YouTube: Search for Microsoft Sway tutorials on YouTube. There are many channels that offer detailed guides, tips, and walkthroughs. Some recommended channels include Microsoft's official channel and popular tech tutorial channels.

2. Udemy: Udemy offers paid courses that provide in-depth training on Microsoft Sway. These courses are often structured to take you from beginner to advanced levels. Look for courses with high ratings and positive reviews.

3. LinkedIn Learning: As part of LinkedIn, this platform offers professional courses on various software, including Sway. These courses are created by experts and are often accompanied by certificates upon completion.

4. Coursera: Similar to Udemy, Coursera provides structured courses that can help you master Sway. These courses are usually created in partnership with universities or professional organizations.

Microsoft TechNet and MSDN

For more technical and in-depth resources, Microsoft TechNet and the Microsoft Developer Network (MSDN) can be very useful:

1. TechNet: TechNet is designed for IT professionals and offers technical documentation, resources, and community support. It's a good place to find detailed information about how Sway integrates with other Microsoft services.

2. MSDN: MSDN caters to developers and includes API documentation, SDKs, and technical articles. If you're looking to develop custom solutions or integrate Sway into other applications, this is the place to go.

Microsoft Learn

Microsoft Learn is an educational platform offering interactive learning paths and modules on various Microsoft products, including Sway:

1. Visit Microsoft Learn: Go to [Microsoft Learn](https://learn.microsoft.com).

2. Search for Sway: Use the search function to find learning paths or modules related to Sway. These interactive tutorials often include hands-on labs and quizzes to test your knowledge.

3. Complete Learning Paths: Learning paths are collections of related modules that provide a comprehensive learning experience. Completing a learning path can give you a well-rounded understanding of Sway.

Third-Party Blogs and Websites

Numerous tech blogs and websites provide tips, tutorials, and troubleshooting guides for Microsoft Sway:

1. Tech Blogs: Websites like TechCrunch, CNET, and The Verge often publish articles on new features and tips for using Sway. These articles can provide insights into the latest updates and practical uses.

2. User Blogs: Personal blogs by tech enthusiasts and educators often share real-world experiences and solutions. Searching for specific problems can lead you to blog posts that address those issues.

3. Educational Websites: Websites like EdTech Magazine and TeachThought provide resources for using Sway in educational settings. These can be valuable if you're using Sway for teaching or school projects.

Social Media and Online Communities

Social media platforms and online communities can be valuable resources for quick tips and peer support:

1. Twitter: Follow hashtags like MicrosoftSway and accounts like @MicrosoftEdu for the latest updates and tips.

2. Reddit: Join subreddits like r/Microsoft and r/Office365. These communities are active with users who share solutions and advice.

3. Facebook Groups: Search for Microsoft Sway user groups. These groups often have members who are quick to help with troubleshooting and tips.

Official Documentation

Microsoft's official documentation is a reliable source for detailed information and technical specifications:

1. Access the Documentation: Visit the [Microsoft Docs](https://docs.microsoft.com) website.

2. Search for Sway: Use the search bar to find documentation related to Sway. This includes user guides, technical details, and integration information.

3. Read Through Sections: The documentation is organized into sections that cover different aspects of using Sway. This can include everything from getting started guides to advanced customization options.

By utilizing these online resources, you can effectively troubleshoot issues, learn new features, and enhance your overall experience with Microsoft Sway. Whether you prefer reading articles, watching videos, or engaging with the community, there's a wealth of information available to support you.

9.3 Staying Updated

9.3.1 Latest Features

Staying updated with the latest features of Microsoft Sway is crucial for users who want to leverage the platform's full potential. Microsoft Sway is continuously evolving, with new features and improvements regularly introduced to enhance user experience, functionality, and performance. This section provides a detailed overview of the latest features in Microsoft Sway, helping you make the most of the platform.

1. Enhanced Design Options

One of the most exciting updates to Microsoft Sway is the enhancement of design options. Users now have access to a broader range of customizable design elements that allow for more personalized and visually appealing presentations.

a. New Design Templates

Microsoft Sway regularly updates its collection of design templates, offering a diverse selection to suit different presentation needs. Whether you're creating a business report, a personal blog, or an educational project, you'll find templates that can be customized to match your content and style. Recent updates include templates specifically designed for interactive storytelling, multimedia presentations, and visual portfolios.

b. Advanced Styling Tools

The styling tools in Sway have been upgraded to provide more control over the appearance of your content. You can now adjust fonts, colors, and backgrounds with greater precision. The introduction of gradient and texture options for backgrounds adds depth and richness to your presentations, allowing for more creative expression.

c. Dynamic Layouts

Sway has introduced new layout options that enhance how content is presented. The addition of dynamic layouts, such as split-screen and grid views, allows users to create more engaging and interactive presentations. These layouts are especially useful for presenting complex information in a visually organized manner.

2. Improved Media Integration

Media integration in Microsoft Sway has been significantly improved, making it easier to incorporate various types of content into your presentations.

a. Enhanced Media Search

The media search feature in Sway has been upgraded to include more comprehensive and refined search capabilities. Users can now search for images, videos, and other media from a wider range of sources, including licensed content from integrated stock photo libraries. The improved search functionality helps you find the perfect media to complement your content quickly.

b. Support for More Media Formats

Recent updates to Sway have expanded support for various media formats. You can now embed and display a broader range of media types, including interactive content such as charts and infographics. This expanded support ensures that you can include rich and diverse media elements in your presentations.

c. Improved Media Editing Tools

The media editing tools in Sway have been enhanced to provide more flexibility and control over your content. You can now crop, resize, and apply filters to images directly within the platform. These tools simplify the process of preparing media for inclusion in your Sway presentations, reducing the need for external editing software.

3. Advanced Collaboration Features

Collaboration has always been a key aspect of Microsoft Sway, and recent updates have introduced several new features to enhance this functionality.

a. Real-Time Collaboration

One of the most notable updates is the introduction of real-time collaboration. Multiple users can now work on the same Sway simultaneously, with changes being reflected instantly for all collaborators. This feature is particularly useful for team projects, allowing for seamless and efficient collaboration.

b. Improved Commenting System

The commenting system within Sway has been improved to facilitate better communication between collaborators. You can now leave comments directly on specific sections of the presentation, making it easier to provide feedback and discuss changes. The enhanced commenting system also includes notification features, so you're alerted to new comments and replies.

c. Version History

Sway now includes a version history feature that allows you to track changes made to your presentation over time. You can review previous versions, compare changes, and revert to earlier versions if needed. This feature is invaluable for maintaining a clear record of edits and ensuring that important content is not lost.

4. Enhanced Accessibility Features

Microsoft Sway continues to improve its accessibility features, ensuring that presentations are usable by everyone, including those with disabilities.

a. Improved Screen Reader Support

Recent updates have enhanced Sway's compatibility with screen readers, making it easier for visually impaired users to navigate and interact with presentations. Screen reader support now includes better text-to-speech functionality and improved description of visual elements.

b. New Accessibility Settings

Sway has introduced new accessibility settings that allow users to customize their experience based on their needs. These settings include options for adjusting text size, contrast, and color schemes to improve readability and usability.

c. Keyboard Shortcuts

To support users who rely on keyboard navigation, Sway has added a range of keyboard shortcuts for common tasks. These shortcuts help users navigate the platform more efficiently and perform actions without relying on a mouse.

5. Integration with Other Microsoft Services

Microsoft Sway has strengthened its integration with other Microsoft services, providing a more seamless and interconnected user experience.

a. Integration with Microsoft Teams

Sway now integrates more deeply with Microsoft Teams, allowing users to share and collaborate on Sway presentations directly within Teams channels. This integration streamlines the workflow for team projects and makes it easier to incorporate Sway content into collaborative discussions.

b. Enhanced Integration with OneDrive

The integration with OneDrive has been improved to support more efficient file management and sharing. You can now access and insert files from your OneDrive account directly into Sway presentations, simplifying the process of including documents and other resources.

c. Support for Microsoft Forms

Sway now supports embedding Microsoft Forms directly into presentations. This feature allows you to create interactive surveys, quizzes, and feedback forms that can be seamlessly integrated into your Sway content. The ability to collect and analyze responses within Sway presentations adds a new level of interactivity and engagement.

6. Performance Enhancements

In addition to new features, Microsoft Sway has also made several performance enhancements to improve the overall user experience.

a. Faster Load Times

Recent updates have optimized the performance of Sway, resulting in faster load times for presentations. This improvement ensures that your content is displayed quickly and smoothly, even for complex and media-rich presentations.

b. Improved Stability

Sway has undergone stability improvements to reduce crashes and errors. The platform is now more reliable, providing a smoother and more consistent experience for users.

c. Enhanced Mobile Experience

The mobile version of Sway has been optimized to provide a better experience on smartphones and tablets. Updates include improved touch navigation, better media handling, and enhanced support for mobile-specific features.

9.3.2 Upcoming Updates

Staying updated with the latest features and upcoming updates in Microsoft Sway is crucial for maximizing your use of the tool. As Microsoft continuously improves its applications, being aware of these changes can help you leverage new functionalities and enhancements to create even more engaging and effective presentations. This section will guide you through understanding how to stay informed about upcoming updates, what to expect from these updates, and how to prepare for them.

Understanding Microsoft's Update Cycle

Microsoft follows a regular update cycle for its Office applications, including Sway. These updates can be broadly categorized into:

1. Major Updates: These are significant releases that introduce new features, substantial changes to the user interface, and major improvements to functionality. Major updates are typically released semi-annually.

2. Minor Updates: These updates include smaller enhancements, bug fixes, and performance improvements. Minor updates are released more frequently, often on a monthly basis.

3. Security Updates: Focused on addressing security vulnerabilities, these updates are crucial for maintaining the integrity and safety of your data. Security updates are released as needed, depending on the nature and severity of the vulnerabilities discovered.

Where to Find Information on Upcoming Updates

To stay informed about upcoming updates, you can utilize several resources provided by Microsoft:

1. Microsoft 365 Roadmap: The Microsoft 365 Roadmap is an excellent resource for tracking the development and release of new features and updates. You can filter the roadmap to focus specifically on Sway and see what updates are currently being developed, in the rollout phase, or recently released.

  - Website: [Microsoft 365 Roadmap](https://www.microsoft.com/en-us/microsoft-365/roadmap)

2. Office Insider Program: By joining the Office Insider Program, you can get early access to new features and updates before they are widely released. This program offers two levels of access:

  - Insider Fast: Provides access to the newest features and updates that are still in development. This level is best for users who want to be on the cutting edge and provide feedback to Microsoft.

  - Insider Slow: Offers access to features and updates that are closer to the final release, making it a more stable option compared to Insider Fast.

  - Join Here: [Office Insider Program](https://insider.office.com/)

3. Microsoft Sway Blog: The official Microsoft Sway blog is another valuable resource. It provides detailed announcements about new features, updates, and tips on how to use Sway more effectively.

  - Blog: [Microsoft Sway Blog](https://techcommunity.microsoft.com/t5/microsoft-sway-blog/bg-p/SwayBlog)

4. Community Forums and User Groups: Participating in community forums and user groups can also keep you informed. These platforms often discuss upcoming updates, share insights, and provide real-world feedback on new features.

  - Microsoft Tech Community: [Tech Community](https://techcommunity.microsoft.com/)

  - Reddit: [r/Office365](https://www.reddit.com/r/Office365/)

What to Expect from Upcoming Updates

Microsoft Sway updates often focus on enhancing usability, improving performance, and adding new features that cater to a wide range of users. Here are some areas where you can expect updates:

1. Enhanced User Interface (UI) and User Experience (UX):

  - Streamlined Design: Updates may include a more intuitive interface, making it easier to navigate and create presentations.

  - Customization Options: Look for new themes, fonts, and layout options to provide greater flexibility in designing your Sways.

2. New Features and Functionalities:

  - Interactive Elements: Microsoft may introduce new interactive features, such as quizzes, polls, or more advanced multimedia embedding options.

  - Collaboration Tools: Enhanced collaboration tools can facilitate better teamwork, allowing multiple users to work on a Sway simultaneously with improved real-time editing and commenting features.

3. Performance Improvements:

  - Speed and Efficiency: Updates often focus on improving the loading times and responsiveness of the application, especially when dealing with large presentations.

  - Cross-Platform Compatibility: Ensuring that Sway performs consistently across different devices and browsers is a key focus of many updates.

4. Integration with Other Microsoft 365 Services:

- Seamless Integration: Expect better integration with other Microsoft 365 applications like Teams, OneNote, and SharePoint, allowing for a more cohesive experience.

- Data Sharing and Embedding: Enhanced capabilities for embedding content from other Microsoft 365 services, such as Excel charts or Word documents, directly into Sway presentations.

Preparing for Upcoming Updates

Staying prepared for updates ensures that you can take full advantage of new features and improvements as soon as they are available. Here are some steps to help you prepare:

1. Regular Backups:

- Always keep your important Sways backed up. Although Microsoft provides cloud storage, maintaining a personal backup can prevent any potential data loss during update rollouts.

2. Stay Informed:

- Regularly check the resources mentioned earlier, such as the Microsoft 365 Roadmap and the Sway blog, to stay updated on upcoming changes.

3. Join the Office Insider Program:

- By joining the Office Insider Program, you can get early access to updates and provide feedback to Microsoft, helping to shape the final release.

4. Training and Tutorials:

- Take advantage of training sessions and tutorials offered by Microsoft to learn about new features. Microsoft often provides detailed guides and videos that can help you understand and utilize new functionalities effectively.

5. Feedback and Participation:

- Provide feedback on new features through the Office Insider Program or community forums. Your input can help Microsoft improve the application and tailor it to better meet user needs.

Maximizing the Benefits of Updates

Once updates are released, here's how you can maximize their benefits:

1. Explore New Features:

   - Take the time to explore and experiment with new features. Incorporate them into your Sway presentations to enhance the quality and interactivity of your content.

2. Update Workflows:

   - Integrate new functionalities into your existing workflows. For instance, use enhanced collaboration tools for team projects or new design elements to make your presentations more engaging.

3. Share Knowledge:

   - If you are part of a team or organization, share your knowledge of new features with your colleagues. Conduct training sessions or create internal documentation to help others benefit from the updates.

4. Stay Proactive:

   - Be proactive in seeking out additional resources and tutorials that can help you make the most of new features. Microsoft often releases detailed documentation and video tutorials alongside major updates.

Conclusion

Staying updated with Microsoft Sway's latest features and upcoming updates is essential for harnessing the full potential of this powerful tool. By utilizing resources like the Microsoft 365 Roadmap, participating in the Office Insider Program, and actively engaging with community forums, you can ensure that you are always informed about the latest developments. Preparing for updates through regular backups, training, and proactive exploration will help you seamlessly integrate new functionalities into your presentations, making them more dynamic and effective. Remember, staying informed and proactive not only enhances your own usage of Sway but also contributes to the broader community by providing valuable feedback and insights to Microsoft.

Appendices

A. Keyboard Shortcuts

Mastering keyboard shortcuts can significantly enhance your productivity when using Microsoft Sway. These shortcuts allow you to navigate through the interface, format content, and execute commands quickly without relying on a mouse. This section will provide a comprehensive guide to the most useful keyboard shortcuts in Microsoft Sway.

1. General Navigation Shortcuts

1.1 Opening and Closing

- Ctrl + N: Create a new Sway

- Ctrl + O: Open an existing Sway

- Ctrl + W: Close the current Sway

- Ctrl + S: Save the current Sway

- Esc: Close dialog boxes or exit the current mode

1.2 Moving Through Your Sway

- Tab: Move to the next element

- Shift + Tab: Move to the previous element

- Arrow Keys: Navigate through the content of your Sway

- Home: Move to the beginning of the Storyline

- End: Move to the end of the Storyline

2. Editing Shortcuts

2.1 Text Editing

- Ctrl + A: Select all text in the current card

- Ctrl + C: Copy selected text

- Ctrl + X: Cut selected text

- Ctrl + V: Paste copied text

- Ctrl + Z: Undo the last action

- Ctrl + Y: Redo the last undone action

- Ctrl + B: Bold the selected text

- Ctrl + I: Italicize the selected text

- Ctrl + U: Underline the selected text

2.2 Formatting and Styling

- Ctrl + E: Center align text

- Ctrl + L: Left align text

- Ctrl + R: Right align text

- Ctrl + Shift + L: Apply bullet points to the selected text

- Ctrl + Shift + N: Apply numbered list to the selected text

3. Media and Card Management

3.1 Adding and Managing Cards

- Ctrl + M: Add a new text card

- Ctrl + Shift + M: Add a new media card

- Ctrl + D: Duplicate the selected card

- Delete: Delete the selected card

3.2 Inserting Media

- Ctrl + Shift + I: Insert an image

- Ctrl + Shift + V: Insert a video

- Ctrl + Shift + E: Insert an embed code

4. Advanced Editing and Customization

4.1 Using the Design and Layout

- Ctrl + Shift + D: Open the Design tab

- Ctrl + Shift + T: Open the Styles pane

- Ctrl + Shift + P: Preview your Sway

4.2 Accessibility Features

- Ctrl + Alt + M: Open the Accessibility Checker

- Ctrl + Alt + N: Navigate to the next section in the Accessibility Checker

- Ctrl + Alt + P: Navigate to the previous section in the Accessibility Checker

5. Collaboration and Sharing

5.1 Managing Permissions

- Ctrl + Shift + C: Open the Share pane

- Ctrl + Shift + R: Set read-only permissions

- Ctrl + Shift + W: Set edit permissions

6. Custom Shortcuts and Tips

6.1 Creating Custom Shortcuts

While Microsoft Sway does not natively support creating custom keyboard shortcuts, you can use third-party tools or operating system features to map custom shortcuts to specific actions. For example, on Windows, you can use AutoHotkey to create scripts that trigger specific Sway commands. On macOS, you can use Automator or Keyboard Maestro for similar functionality.

6.2 Tips for Efficient Workflow

1. Combine Shortcuts: Learn to combine shortcuts to streamline your workflow. For instance, after pasting text with Ctrl + V, quickly format it with Ctrl + B for bold or Ctrl + I for italics.

2. Use Preview Often: Regularly preview your Sway with Ctrl + Shift + P to ensure your design and content are aligning as expected.

3. Master Navigation: Efficient navigation with Tab, Shift + Tab, and the arrow keys can save time, especially in large Sways with many cards.

7. Platform-Specific Shortcuts

7.1 Windows Shortcuts

While most shortcuts work across platforms, there are a few that are specific to Windows:

- Alt + F4: Close the Sway application

- Ctrl + Shift + Esc: Open the Task Manager to troubleshoot performance issues

7.2 macOS Shortcuts

For macOS users, some shortcuts may differ slightly:

- Command + N: Create a new Sway

- Command + O: Open an existing Sway

- Command + W: Close the current Sway

- Command + S: Save the current Sway

- Command + Z: Undo the last action

- Command + Shift + Z: Redo the last undone action

- Command + B: Bold the selected text

- Command + I: Italicize the selected text

- Command + U: Underline the selected text

8. Troubleshooting and Optimization

8.1 Troubleshooting Shortcut Issues

If you find that certain shortcuts are not working:

1. Check Keyboard Settings: Ensure that your keyboard layout and settings are correctly configured in your operating system.

2. Application Focus: Make sure Sway is the active application when using shortcuts.

3. Conflicting Software: Some software can override keyboard shortcuts. Close unnecessary applications to prevent conflicts.

8.2 Optimizing Keyboard Usage

1. Practice Regularly: Frequent use of keyboard shortcuts will help you memorize them and improve your efficiency.

2. Keep a Cheat Sheet: Create a list of the most commonly used shortcuts and keep it near your workstation for quick reference.

3. Use Keyboard Shortcuts Consistently: Develop a habit of using shortcuts for every action, reducing your reliance on the mouse and speeding up your workflow.

Conclusion

Keyboard shortcuts are powerful tools that can enhance your efficiency and productivity when using Microsoft Sway. By mastering these shortcuts, you can streamline your workflow, create more dynamic presentations, and manage your content with ease. Remember to practice regularly and incorporate these shortcuts into your daily use of Sway to fully benefit from their potential.

B. Glossary of Terms

In this section, we provide definitions and explanations of key terms and concepts related to Microsoft Sway. This glossary aims to help beginners understand the terminology used throughout the application and in this tutorial.

A

Accessibility: Features in Microsoft Sway that ensure content can be accessed by all users, including those with disabilities. Examples include screen reader compatibility and alt text for images.

Account: A Microsoft account required to use Sway. It allows users to create, edit, and share Sway presentations.

Alignment: The arrangement of text and objects within a Sway card or across the entire presentation. Proper alignment ensures that the content is visually appealing and easy to read.

Alt Text: Short for alternative text, alt text is a description of an image or media used to make content accessible to people using screen readers. It is an essential component of web accessibility.

B

Background Image: An image used as the backdrop of a Sway presentation. It helps set the theme and tone of the content. Users can customize the background image to enhance the visual appeal of their Sway.

Block: A section within a Sway presentation that contains content such as text, images, or videos. Blocks help organize information and make the presentation more structured.

Bookmark: A feature that allows users to mark a specific section or card within a Sway for easy reference later. It helps in navigating lengthy presentations.

Branding: Customizing a Sway presentation to reflect a particular brand's identity, including using specific colors, logos, and fonts. This is useful for corporate presentations and marketing materials.

C

Card: The basic building block of a Sway presentation. Each card contains a piece of content, such as text, images, videos, or embedded content. Cards can be rearranged to change the order of the presentation.

Collaboration: The ability to work with others on the same Sway presentation in real-time. This feature is essential for teamwork and ensures that multiple users can contribute to a project simultaneously.

Content: The information and media included in a Sway presentation. This can be text, images, videos, audio files, or embedded web content.

CSS (Cascading Style Sheets): A style sheet language used to describe the look and formatting of a document written in HTML. In Sway, users can use CSS to customize the design and layout of their presentations.

D

Dashboard: The main screen where users can view, create, and manage their Sway presentations. It provides access to all the tools and features needed to work with Sway.

Design Tab: A section in the Sway interface that allows users to choose and customize the visual style of their presentation. It includes options for themes, layouts, and color schemes.

Drag and Drop: A method of interacting with the user interface by dragging items with a mouse or touch screen and dropping them into a new location. This feature makes it easy to rearrange cards and add new content to a Sway presentation.

E

Embed: To insert content from another website or application into a Sway presentation. Examples include embedding YouTube videos, tweets, and maps. This feature enriches the presentation with interactive and dynamic content.

Export: The process of saving a Sway presentation in a different format, such as PDF or Word. Exporting allows users to share their presentations in formats that can be viewed offline or printed.

F

Font: The style and appearance of text used in a Sway presentation. Users can choose from various fonts to match the presentation's theme and enhance readability.

Formatting: The process of arranging and styling text and other content within a Sway card. This includes setting font size, color, alignment, and adding bullet points or numbered lists.

G

Group Card: A type of card in Sway that allows users to group multiple pieces of content together. This is useful for organizing related information and creating visually appealing sections within a presentation.

Grid: A layout option in Sway that arranges content in a grid format. It is particularly useful for displaying images and other media in a structured and organized manner.

H

Header: The top section of a Sway card that typically contains the title or main heading. Headers help organize the presentation and guide the audience through the content.

Hyperlink: A link to a web page, document, or another part of the same presentation. Hyperlinks allow users to create interactive and connected content within their Sway.

I

Image: A visual representation included in a Sway card. Images can be uploaded from a user's device or sourced from the web using Sway's built-in search features.

Import: The process of bringing content from external sources into Sway. This includes importing text from Word documents, images from a device, or videos from YouTube.

J

Journal: A type of Sway presentation used for documenting and sharing personal experiences, such as travel journals or daily logs. Journals can include text, images, and other media to create a comprehensive record.

K

Keyword: A significant word or phrase used in the search and organization of content within Sway. Keywords help users find and categorize information efficiently.

L

Layout: The arrangement of content within a Sway card or across the entire presentation. Different layouts can be used to emphasize particular pieces of content or create a specific visual flow.

Link: A reference to a web page or another part of the same presentation. Links can be embedded in text or images and provide a way to navigate between related content.

M

Media: Various types of content that can be included in a Sway presentation, such as images, videos, audio files, and embedded web content. Media enhances the presentation by making it more engaging and interactive.

Mobile View: The layout of a Sway presentation when viewed on a mobile device. Sway automatically adjusts the design to be mobile-friendly, ensuring that content is accessible and readable on smaller screens.

N

Navigation Pane: A tool in the Sway interface that allows users to move through their presentation easily. It provides an overview of the cards and helps users jump to specific sections quickly.

O

Orientation: The direction in which content is displayed in a Sway presentation. Sway supports both horizontal and vertical orientations, allowing users to choose the best format for their content.

P

Preview: A feature that allows users to see how their Sway presentation will look to the audience. Previewing helps identify any adjustments needed before sharing or presenting.

Publish: The process of making a Sway presentation available to others. Publishing can include sharing a link, embedding the presentation in a website, or exporting it to another format.

Q

Quick Start: A set of pre-designed templates and tools in Sway that help users create presentations quickly. Quick Start options provide a foundation that users can customize with their own content.

R

Remix: A feature in Sway that automatically applies a new design and layout to a presentation. Remixing allows users to experiment with different styles and find the best look for their content.

Responsive Design: An approach to web design that ensures content looks good on all devices, from desktops to mobile phones. Sway's responsive design adapts presentations to fit different screen sizes.

S

Storyboard: A visual representation of the sequence of cards in a Sway presentation. The storyboard helps users plan and organize their content effectively.

Style: The overall look and feel of a Sway presentation, including colors, fonts, and layout options. Users can choose from various styles to match their content and audience.

T

Template: A pre-designed layout and style that users can apply to their Sway presentations. Templates help streamline the creation process by providing a foundation that users can build upon.

Theme: A collection of design elements, including colors, fonts, and backgrounds, that give a Sway presentation a cohesive look. Themes can be customized to match the presentation's content and purpose.

U

User Interface (UI): The visual elements and controls that users interact with in Sway. The UI includes menus, buttons, and tools that help users create and manage their presentations.

URL: The web address of a Sway presentation. Sharing the URL allows others to view the presentation online.

V

Video: A type of media that can be included in a Sway presentation. Videos can be uploaded from a device or embedded from online sources like YouTube.

View Mode: The way a Sway presentation is displayed to the audience. View mode differs from edit mode, where users make changes to their content.

W

Web Content: Any content from the internet that can be embedded in a Sway presentation. This includes videos, social media posts, maps, and other online resources.

Workflow: The series of steps and processes involved in creating a Sway presentation. Understanding the workflow helps users organize their tasks and produce high-quality content efficiently.

X

XML: A markup language used for encoding documents in a format that is both human-readable and machine-readable. While not directly used in Sway, understanding XML can be helpful for advanced users working with web content and embeds.

Y

YouTube: A popular video-sharing platform where users can find and embed videos into their Sway presentations. Embedding YouTube videos enhances the presentation with dynamic content.

Z

Zoom: A feature that allows users to enlarge or reduce the view of their Sway presentation. Zooming helps in editing specific details and ensures that the overall layout is visually appealing.

C. Conclusion

As we conclude our journey through the vast and innovative world of Microsoft Sway, it's important to reflect on the immense capabilities and potential that this tool offers. From creating dynamic presentations to crafting engaging narratives, Microsoft Sway stands out as a versatile platform that bridges the gap between traditional slideshows and interactive digital storytelling.

Throughout this guide, we've explored the fundamental aspects of using Microsoft Sway, beginning with the basics and gradually advancing to more sophisticated features. By now, you should feel confident in your ability to navigate the Sway interface, create and customize content, and share your work with others. Let's revisit some of the key takeaways from each chapter:

Chapter 1: Introduction to Microsoft Sway

We started with an introduction to Microsoft Sway, where we discussed its unique position in the realm of presentation tools. Unlike traditional slide-based software, Sway offers a more fluid and interactive approach, allowing users to create visually appealing presentations without extensive design skills. We highlighted the benefits of using Sway, including its ease of use, cloud-based accessibility, and seamless integration with other Microsoft services.

Chapter 2: Navigating the Sway Interface

In this chapter, we delved into the Sway dashboard, exploring the different components that make up the interface. We learned about the Storyline and Design tabs, which serve as the primary areas for creating and customizing your Sway. The navigation pane and preview options were also covered, providing you with the tools to effectively manage and review your content.

Chapter 3: Creating Your First Sway

Creating a new Sway from scratch or using a template was the focus of this chapter. We walked through the process of adding various types of content, such as text, media, and group cards. The importance of customizing your Sway to fit your audience and purpose was emphasized, along with practical tips for making your presentation engaging and cohesive.

Chapter 4: Working with Text and Media

This chapter provided a deep dive into the rich media capabilities of Sway. We explored how to add and format text, insert images and videos, and embed external content such as maps and social media posts. By understanding how to leverage these features, you can create more dynamic and interactive presentations that capture your audience's attention.

Chapter 5: Design and Layout Customization

Design and layout customization are crucial for creating visually appealing Sways. In this chapter, we discussed the various design themes available in Sway and how to apply custom design options. We also covered the differences between vertical and horizontal layouts and provided advanced techniques for grouping and aligning cards to create a polished final product.

Chapter 6: Sharing and Collaborating

Sharing your Sway with others and collaborating on projects were the main topics of this chapter. We examined the different sharing settings, how to generate a shareable link, and the collaboration features that allow multiple users to work on a Sway simultaneously. Additionally, we looked at exporting and printing options for those who need to present their Sway offline.

Chapter 7: Advanced Features and Tips

In this chapter, we explored some of the more advanced features of Sway, including analytics, accessibility options, and various tips and tricks for creating effective presentations.

Understanding these advanced features can help you take full advantage of Sway's capabilities and ensure that your presentations are both impactful and inclusive.

Chapter 8: Use Cases for Microsoft Sway

To provide practical applications of Sway, we discussed various use cases across different fields. Whether you're an educator looking to create interactive lessons, a business professional crafting marketing presentations, or an individual planning a personal event, Sway offers a range of tools to suit your needs. By exploring these use cases, you can better understand how to tailor your Sway presentations to your specific context.

Chapter 9: Troubleshooting and Support

Finally, we addressed common issues that users may encounter when using Sway and provided solutions to these problems. Accessing Microsoft support resources and staying updated with the latest features and updates were also discussed, ensuring that you have the necessary tools and knowledge to maintain and improve your Sway presentations over time.

Reflecting on Your Learning Journey

As you reflect on your learning journey with Microsoft Sway, it's important to recognize the progress you've made. Transitioning from a beginner to a confident user involves not only mastering the technical aspects of the tool but also understanding how to effectively communicate your ideas through engaging and interactive presentations.

By experimenting with different features, layouts, and design elements, you can develop a unique style that resonates with your audience. Remember that creating impactful presentations is as much about storytelling as it is about design. Focus on conveying your message clearly and concisely, while also making use of Sway's multimedia capabilities to enhance your narrative.

Future Opportunities with Microsoft Sway

Looking ahead, consider how you can continue to utilize Microsoft Sway in your personal and professional endeavors. The skills and knowledge you've gained from this guide will serve as a strong foundation for creating compelling presentations across various contexts. Whether you're presenting to colleagues, clients, students, or friends, Sway offers a flexible and powerful platform to showcase your ideas.

Stay curious and open to new features and updates from Microsoft. As technology evolves, so too will the capabilities of Sway, providing you with even more tools to create and share your stories. Engage with the Sway community, seek inspiration from others, and continue to push the boundaries of what's possible with this innovative tool.

Acknowledgments

We extend our heartfelt gratitude to all readers of "Microsoft Sway: The Complete Tutorial for Beginners." Your decision to invest in this book is a testament to your commitment to learning and improving your presentation skills. We hope that this guide has provided you with valuable insights and practical knowledge to confidently use Microsoft Sway in your endeavors.

To our readers who are educators, thank you for your dedication to enhancing the learning experiences of your students. We believe that Sway can be a powerful tool in the classroom, fostering creativity and engagement among learners. Your efforts in integrating technology into education are truly commendable.

To the business professionals, we appreciate your pursuit of excellence in your presentations and reports. Microsoft Sway offers a dynamic platform to convey complex information in an accessible and visually appealing manner. We hope this guide has equipped you with the skills to create impactful presentations that drive results.

To all individuals using Sway for personal projects, thank you for embracing this tool to share your stories, events, and ideas. Your creativity and enthusiasm are what make Sway such a versatile and inspiring platform. We are grateful for the opportunity to be a part of your journey.

A special thank you goes to the Microsoft Sway development team for creating such an innovative and user-friendly tool. Your dedication to improving digital storytelling and presentation software has made a significant impact on how people share their ideas and connect with others.

Finally, we extend our deepest appreciation to our families, friends, and colleagues who have supported us throughout the writing of this book. Your encouragement, feedback, and patience have been invaluable, and we are grateful for your unwavering support.

Final Thoughts

As you continue to explore and utilize Microsoft Sway, remember that the key to effective presentations lies in the seamless integration of content, design, and interaction. Use the knowledge and skills gained from this guide to create presentations that not only inform but also inspire and engage your audience.

Thank you once again for choosing "Microsoft Sway: The Complete Tutorial for Beginners." We wish you all the best in your future presentations and storytelling endeavors. Keep creating, keep sharing, and keep pushing the boundaries of what's possible with Microsoft Sway.

Happy Swaying!